Patent Damages

An Economic Framework for Lawyers

Gregory J. Urbanchuk

AMERICAN BAR ASSOCIATION
Intellectual Property
Law Section

Cover design by Jill Tedhams/ABA Design

Printed in the United States of America.

30 29 28 27 26 5 4 3 2 1

ISBN 978-1-63905-762-7

Discounts are available for books ordered in bulk. Special consideration is given to state bars, CLE programs, and other bar-related organizations. Inquire at Book Publishing, ABA Publishing, American Bar Association, 321 N. Clark Street, Chicago, Illinois 60654-7598.

www.shopABA.org

Dedication

For my kids:

Alexander

Addison

Contents

About the Author

Gregory J. Urbanchuk, MSc., CVA, is a principal in the Forensics, Litigation, and Valuation Group at Grassi, where he leads the firm's Intellectual Property Services. He has over 20 years of experience providing forensic, dispute, valuation, and intellectual property consulting services in the United States, the United Kingdom, and Europe. Previously, Mr. Urbanchuk worked for boutique, regional, and national consulting firms, including Deloitte LLP in London.

Mr. Urbanchuk serves as an expert witness in complex commercial litigation in the area of intellectual property damages and valuation. He has evaluated damages and testified in cases claiming patent, trademark, and copyright infringement; the misappropriation of trade secrets; and the valuation of intellectual property. Mr. Urbanchuk has significant experience analyzing damages using lost profits, reasonable royalty, and disgorgement theories of recovery.

Outside of litigation, Mr. Urbanchuk values public and privately held businesses and intellectual property in connection with mergers and acquisitions, financial reporting, taxation, and estate planning. He has significant expertise in the valuation of intellectual property, including patents, trademarks, copyrights, trade secrets, brands, license agreements, software, and customer and vendor relationships, among others. Mr. Urbanchuk has provided valuation services in numerous industries such as life sciences, healthcare, technology, consumer, manufacturing, and financial services.

His writing has appeared in numerous publications such as the *Oxford Journal of Intellectual Property Law and Practice*, *Les Nouvelles*, *International Company and Commercial Law Review*, *Computer & Internet Lawyer*, *Intellectual Property Litigation*, and *IP Litigator*.

Mr. Urbanchuk has a master of science by research with distinction in international business from the University of London, where he authored a dissertation on patent enforcement rules and economic damages.

Chapter 1
Introduction

Expert Testimony

Quantifying monetary relief in patent cases starts with a fundamental question: What is expert testimony?

Federal Rule of Evidence 702 states:[1]

> A witness who is qualified as an expert by knowledge, skill, experience, training, or education may testify in the form of an opinion or otherwise if the proponent demonstrates to the court that it is more likely than not that: (a) the expert's scientific, technical, or other specialized knowledge will help the trier of fact to understand the evidence or to determine a fact in issue; (b) the testimony is based on sufficient facts or data; (c) the testimony is the product of reliable principles and methods; and (d) the expert's opinion reflects a reliable application of the principles and methods to the facts of the case.

As noted by the Third Circuit, Federal Rule of Evidence 702 places three restrictions on expert testimony: (1) qualification, (2) reliability, and (3) fit.[2] Qualification requires the expert to have specialized expertise. The Federal Circuit interprets the qualification requirement liberally, stating that "a broad range of knowledge, skills, and training qualify an expert."[3] Reliability requires an expert to base testimony on "the 'methods and procedures of science' rather than on 'subjective belief or unsupported

---

1. Fed. R. Evid. 702(a), (c).
2. Schneider *ex rel.* Estate of Schneider v. Fried, 320 F.3d 396, 404 (3d Cir. 2003).
3. *Id.* at 404 (citing *In re* Paoli Railroad Yard PCB Litigation, 35 F.3d 741 (3d Cir. 1994)).

speculation'; the expert must have 'good grounds' for his or her belief."[4] Fit requires that expert testimony is relevant to the issues in the case and assists the trier of fact.[5] Acting as a gatekeeper, the district court prevents testimony that fails the requirements of qualification, reliability, and fit at a "*Daubert* hearing."[6]

Increased Complexity of Expert Testimony

The number of new patent cases filed in U.S. District Courts decreased from approximately 5,400 in 2021 to 4,300 in 2023.[7] While new filings decreased, the complexity of patent cases continued to increase. This increase in complexity is, in part, due to the uncertainty related to the quantification of monetary relief arising from patent infringement.

The U.K. High Court cleverly captured the complexity of quantifying monetary relief in *Gerber Garment Technology Inc. v. Lectra Systems Ltd.*, stating:[8]

> When I first looked at the accountants' various reports, supplementary reports, and further supplementary reports, I thought they were counting the uncountable; assuming the unreliable as sands on which to build towers of detailed calculation. I still think this is largely so. . . . Although I have had to reach an answer I do not pretend it is an accurate measure of the damage, of what would have been. It is just the best assessment I can make.

Decided *Daubert* motions related to economic experts directly demonstrate the impact of complexity on the quantification of monetary relief in patent cases. Between 2019 and 2023, 70 percent of decided *Daubert* motions related to economic experts occurred in five districts: the District of Delaware, the Eastern District of Texas, the Western District of Texas, the Northern District of California, and the Northern District of

4. *Id.* at 404.
5. *Id.*
6. *Id.*
7. Statistics obtained from Docket Navigator.
8. Gerber Garment Tech. Inc. v. Lectra Systems Ltd. [1995] R.P.C. 383.

Illinois.[9] Over 50 percent of the decided *Daubert* motions partially or fully excluded economic experts on issues involving monetary relief.[10] The preceding indicates that quantifying monetary relief for patent damages is equivalent to a coin flip. This raises an important question: How can you ensure your economic expert provides a reliable, supportable quantification of monetary relief? This book attempts to answer that question.

Organization

Chapters 2 to 8 of this book present a framework for identifying, choosing, and applying the methodologies used to quantify the available monetary remedies arising from patent infringement claims. The framework is a guide. It provides a mechanism that, if followed, reduces complexity and ensures that your economic expert presents a reliable and defensible quantification of monetary relief.

Chapter 2 addresses the normative or optimal economic model of monetary relief arising from patent infringement claims. This chapter covers the purpose of a patent, the patent incentive, general theories of monetary relief, and the development of the normative model.

Chapter 3 addresses the U.S. statutory provisions governing the quantification of monetary relief arising from patent infringement claims. This chapter covers the statutory provisions for utility and design patents, as well as the determination of the damage period.

Chapter 4 addresses the choice between lost profits and reasonable royalty methodologies. This chapter covers the entitlement to lost profits, the Panduit Test, and the Two-Supplier Market Test.

Chapters 5, 6, and 7 address the quantification of monetary relief. Chapter 5 addresses the quantification of monetary relief using a lost profits methodology. This chapter covers (1) the components of lost revenue (two and multi-supplier markets), which include infringing sales, price erosion, and convoyed sales, and (2) incremental costs, which include a consideration of variable and fixed cost behaviors, and the relationship

9. Statistics obtained from Docket Navigator.

10. *Id.*

between marginal and incremental costs. Chapter 6 addresses the quantification of monetary relief using a reasonable royalty methodology. This chapter covers three approaches used by the courts to quantify a reasonable royalty: (1) established royalty, (2) hypothetical negotiation, and (3) the analytical method. Chapter 7 addresses the quantification of monetary relief using the defendant's profits methodology, which remains an available form of recovery for design patents.

Finally, Chapter 8 addresses apportionment. This chapter covers apportionment requirements for lost profits, reasonable royalties, and defendant's profits.

Chapters 9 to 11 of this book serve as a toolkit, providing additional information on financial and economic concepts related to patent infringement claims.

Chapter 9 addresses the income statement. This chapter covers (1) levels of income statements (i.e., company, divisional, and product) and (2) the related guidance for patent damages.

Chapter 10 addresses the generally accepted patent valuation approaches and methods and their applicability to a reasonable royalty methodology.

Chapter 11 addresses discount rates used in a valuation using the Income Approach, a generally accepted patent valuation approach.

Chapter 12 addresses pre-judgment interest concepts, including the difference between simple and compounding interest, and the impact of compounding.

Chapter 13 addresses purchase price allocations and royalty rates. This chapter covers the theory of purchase price allocations and their use in damage analysis under a reasonable royalty methodology.

Chapter 2
Normative Economic Model

This chapter addresses the normative or optimal economic model of monetary relief arising from patent infringement claims.

Patent protection provides an incentive to the patent holder for the time, risk, and cost of developing a new technology. The disclosure of patented technology adds to society's collective knowledge by enabling access. The strength and availability of monetary relief are factors that impact this incentive/access balance.

An economic consideration of a firm's patent "incentive" provides a starting point for the normative or optimal model of monetary relief. Two general theories of monetary relief used by the courts are (1) damages and (2) restitution.

The normative or optimal economic model of monetary relief deters infringement by making it unprofitable. Therefore, under a normative or optimal economic model of monetary relief for patent infringement, a patent holder should be entitled to the greater of its but for damages attributable to the infringement or the defendant's profits from the use of the infringing technology.

The Purpose of a Patent

In the U.S., there are three types of patents.[1] Utility patents are "for inventing a new or improved and useful process, machine, article of manufacture, or composition of matter."[2] Design patents are "for inventing a new, original, and ornamental design for an article of manufacture."[3]

1. USPTO, *Patent Essentials* (June 5, 2024, 3:43 p.m.), https://www.uspto.gov/patents/basics/essentials#questions.

2. *Id.*

3. *Id.*

Plant patents are "for inventing or discovering and asexually reproducing any distinct and new variety of plant."[4] A patent gives an inventor the "right to 'exclude others from making, using, offering for sale, or selling' an invention or 'importing' it into the U.S."[5]

In general, a patent provides a limited term of protection to an inventor in return for access to the details of the patented technology. As noted in *The Economic Structure of Intellectual Property Law*, "[T]he standard rationale of patent law is that it is an efficient method of enabling the benefits of research and development to be internalized, thus promoting innovation and technological progress."[6] On one hand, patent protection rewards an inventor for the time, risk, and cost of developing new technology, thus providing an incentive for future innovation. On the other hand, disclosure of the patented technology adds to society's collective knowledge and is available for use by all after the patent expires.

Several factors impact this incentive/access balance and the strength of patent rights, including (1) length of the patent term, (2) subject matter of patents (i.e., what can and cannot be patented), (3) scope of protection (i.e., broad versus narrow rights), and (4) the strength and availability of remedies to prevent and compensate for infringement.[7]

The Patent Incentive

Developing a normative or optimal model of monetary relief resulting from patent infringement begins with an economic consideration of a firm's patent incentive (i.e., the decision to invest in a new technology).[8] A firm or inventor will invest in a patent if the present value of the future expected cash flows exceeds the present value of future research and development costs.[9]

---

4. *Id.* (This book does not address plant patents.)

5. *Id.*

6. W.M. Landes & R.A. Posner, The Economic Structure of Intellectual Property Law 294 (Harvard University Press 2003).

7. *Id.* at 294–333.

8. R.D. Blair & T.G. Cotter, Intellectual Property: Economics and Legal Dimensions of Rights and Remedies 44 (Cambridge University Press 2005).

9. *Id.*

For example, an inventor estimates that developing a patented technology will cost $100,000 in research and development (R&D) in year one. The inventor believes the patented technology will have an economic useful life of five years and will generate annual cash flows of $50,000 in years two to five. Should the investor invest? In this simplified example, yes.

The following illustration indicates a patent incentive, as the net present value is greater than zero (i.e., the present value of the expected cash flows exceeds the present value of the expected R&D costs).

Patent Incentive: Net Present Value > 0						
		Year				
		1	**2**	**3**	**4**	**5**
Expected Cash Flow	[1]	$—	$ 50,000	$ 50,000	$ 50,000	$ 50,000
R&D Costs	[2]	$ (100,000)	$—	$—	$—	$—
Net Cash Flow	[3]=[1]+[2]	$ (100,000)	$ 50,000	$ 50,000	$ 50,000	$ 50,000
Discount Rate	[4]	18.0%	18.0%	18.0%	18.0%	18.0%
Discount Periods	[5]	0.50	1.50	2.50	3.50	4.50
Present Value Interest Factor	[6]=1/(1+[4])^[5]	0.9206	0.7801	0.6611	0.5603	0.4748
Present Value	[7]=[3]*[6]	$ (92,060)	$ 39,005	$ 33,055	$ 28,015	$ 23,740
Net Present Value	[8]=Σ[7]					$ 31,755

General Theories of Monetary Relief

Two major monetary remedies the courts use include (1) damages and (2) restitution.[10] The distinction between these monetary remedies provides a basis for considering the normative economic or optimal economic model of monetary relief for patent infringement.

Damages and restitution are economically distinct. However, economic experts, attorneys, and courts often interchangeably use the terms "damages" and "restitution."

10. Dan Dobbs & Caprice Roberts, Law of Remedies (Hornbooks) § 1.1 (West Academic, Kindle ed.).

As noted in the *Law of Remedies*:[11]

> The concepts of restitution and damages are quite distinct, but sometimes courts use the term damages when they mean restitution. The two concepts may be further confused by the fact that the amount of defendant's gains may furnish some evidence about plaintiff's probable losses. But again, the damages remedy and the restitutionary remedies are always conceptually distinct and often distinct in dollar amount as well.

The *AICPA Forensic & Valuation Practice Aid: Calculating Lost Profits* also recognizes the economic distinction between damages and restitution, noting:[12]

> a disgorgement of the wrongdoer's profits, which is sometimes referred to as restitution, unjust enrichment, or ill-gotten gains. This measure (which is sometimes referred to as damages but more precisely is a monetary remedy, but not "damages") is focused on the benefit obtained by the defendant.

The economic goal of damages is to compensate a plaintiff for their actual losses.[13] Compensatory damages for patent infringement include lost profits and reasonable royalties. They exist in the but for world. For example, the lost profits on sales that the plaintiff would have made but for the defendant's wrongful actions.

Conversely, the economic goal of restitution is to prevent unjust enrichment by requiring the return of the defendant's gains.[14] Disgorgement of the defendant's profits is a common form of restitution.[15]

---

11. *Id.* § 3.1.
12. Forensic & Valuation Practice Aid: Calculating Lost Profits 12 (AICPA, 2019).
13. Dobbs & Roberts, *supra* note 10.
14. *Id.*
15. Amanda Frye, *"Inextricably Commingled": A Restitution Perspective in Patent Remedies*, 26(2) Harv. J. Law & Tech. 671 (2013).

Normative Economic Model Deters Infringement

Protecting the patent incentive requires establishing monetary relief rules that preserve the net present value by restoring the patent holder to the position it would have been in but for the infringement (i.e., through compensation) or by deterring infringement altogether.[16] Simply stated, to deter infringement, it must be made unprofitable.[17]

As noted in *Intellectual Property: Economics and Legal Dimensions of Rights and Remedies*:[18]

> when there are no substitutes for the patented product and all information, litigation, risk and transaction costs are zero, the optimal damage rules are as follows. First, when the infringers' use of the patent is no more efficient than the patentee's, the minimum sanction should be the restitution of the profit attributable to the infringement. Second, when the infringer is the more efficient user, the minimum sanction should be the amount of the royalty the patentee and infringer would have agreed upon ex ante.

In other words, under a normative or optimal economic model of monetary relief for patent infringement, a patent holder should be entitled to the greater of its but for damages attributable to the infringement or the defendant's profits from the use of the infringing technology.

---

16. Blair & Cotter, *supra* note 8, at 44–45.
17. *Id.* at 45.
18. *Id.* at 57.

Chapter 3
Statutory Provisions

Chapter 2 addressed the normative or optimal economic model of monetary relief for patent infringement, where a patent holder is awarded the greater of its but for damages attributable to the infringement or the defendant's profits from the use of the infringing technology.

This chapter addresses the forms of monetary relief for the infringement of utility and design patents under current U.S. statutory law.[1]

Before 1946, the U.S. statutory law for monetary relief for the infringement of a utility patent was consistent with the normative or optimal economic model and provided for the recovery of the plaintiff's damages and the defendant's profits. The Patent Act of 1946 eliminated the recovery of the defendant's profits as a form of monetary relief for utility patents. Currently, 35 U.S.C. § 284 only provides for the recovery of "damages adequate to compensate for infringement" of a utility patent, but not less than a "reasonable royalty for the use made of the invention by the infringer."

In addition to actual damages and/or reasonable royalties, 35 U.S.C. § 289 provides an additional remedy for the infringement of a design patent in the form of the defendant's profits.

U.S. statutory law also addresses the damage period. 35 U.S.C. § 286 provides for a six-year damage period, which may be further reduced based on the patent marking rules in 35 U.S.C. § 287.

1. See Appendix 1 for selected United States Code sections related to patent remedies.

Statutory Provisions for Utility Patents

Evolution of Historical Statutory Provisions and the Elimination of Defendant's Profits

Before 1946, U.S. statutory law for monetary relief for utility patent infringement conformed to the normative model. The Patent Act of 1870 entitled a plaintiff: [2]

> to recover, in addition to the profits to be accounted for by the defendant, the damages the complainant has sustained thereby, and the court shall assess the same or cause the same to be assessed under its direction, and the court shall have the same powers to increase the same in its discretion that are given by this act to increase the damages found by verdicts in actions upon the case.

While the Patent Act of 1870 provided for disgorgement of the defendant's profits —a form of restitution—the courts struggled with the concept of apportionment.[3] Apportionment determines the portion of the defendant's profits attributable to the patented technology versus other non-infringing elements. As noted by the Supreme Court in *Garretson v. Clark & Another*, the patentee:[4]

> must in every case give evidence tending to separate or apportion the defendant's profits and the patentee's damages between the patented feature and the unpatented features, and such evidence must be reliable and tangible, and not conjectural or speculative; or he must show, by equally reliable and satisfactory evidence, that the profits and damages are to be calculated on the whole machine, for the reason that the entire value of the whole machine, as a marketable article, is properly and legally attributable to the patented feature.

---

2. Patent Act of 1870, ch. 230, 16 Stat. 198–217 (July 8, 1870), SEC 55.
3. Caprice L. Roberts, *The Case for Restitution and Unjust Enrichment Remedies in Patent Law*, 14(2) Lewis & Clark L. Rev. 659 (2009).
4. Garretson v. Clark & Another, 111 U.S. 120, 121 (1884).

The problem of apportionment for the defendant's profits remedy continued until 1946.[5] The Patent Act of 1946 eliminated all references to the defendant's profits remedy. Despite the preceding, courts were not clear that the Patent Act of 1946 prevented the recovery of the defendant's profits. The Supreme Court decided the ambiguity related to the recoverability of defendant's profits in *Aro Manufacturing Co., Inc., et al. v. Convertible Top Replacement Co., Inc.*, stating that the "present statutory rule is that only 'damages' may be recovered."[6] In reaching its opinion, the Supreme Court quoted the legislative history of the Patent Act of 1946, which stated:[7]

> The object of the bill is to make the basis of recovery in patent infringement suits general damages, that is, any damages the complainant can prove, not less than a reasonable royalty together with interest from the time infringement occurred, rather than profits and damages.

Current Statutory Provisions

35 U.S.C. § 284 addresses the available monetary remedies for the infringement of a utility patent.

Per 35 U.S.C. § 284:

> Upon finding for the claimant the court shall award the claimant damages adequate to compensate for the infringement, but in no event less than a reasonable royalty for the use made of the invention by the infringer, together with interest and costs as fixed by the court.
>
> When the damages are not found by a jury, the court shall assess them. In either event the court may increase the damages of up to three times the amount found or assessed.
>
> The court may receive expert testimony as an aid to the determination of damages or of what royalty would be reasonable under the circumstances.

---

5. Roberts, *supra* note 3, at 659–60.
6. Aro Mfg. Co., Inc., et al. v. Convertible Top Replacement Co., Inc., 377 U.S. 476, 507 (1964).
7. *Id.* at 505–06.

The Federal Circuit described the "statutory standard" for quantifying patent damages, stating:[8]

> The question to be asked in determining damages is "how much had the Patent Holder and Licensee suffered by the infringement. And, that question [is] primarily: had the infringer not infringed, what would the Patent Holder-Licensee have made?"

Statutory Provisions for Design Patents

In addition to actual damages and/or reasonable royalties, 35 U.S.C. § 289 provides an additional remedy for the infringement of a design patent.

Per 35 U.S.C. § 289:

> Whoever during the term of a patent for a design, without license of the owner, (1) applies the patented design, or any colorable imitation thereof, to any article of manufacture for the purpose of sale, or (2) sells or exposes for sale any article of manufacture to which such design or colorable imitation has been applied shall be liable to the owner to the extent of his total profit, but not less than $250, recoverable in any United States district court having jurisdiction of the parties.

Unlike utility patents, the current statute for design patents also provides for the recovery of the defendant's profits, which is consistent with the normative model.

Damage Period

35 U.S.C. § 286 places a "time limitation" for recovering monetary relief for the infringement of utility and design patents.

8. Rite-Hite Corp. v. Kelley Co., Inc., 56 F.3d 1545 (Fed. Cir. 1995) (citing Aro Mfg. Co. v. Convertible Top Replacement Co., 377 U.S. 476, 84 S. Ct. 1526, 12 L. Ed. 2d 457, 141 USPQ 681 (1964)).

Per 35 U.S.C. § 286:

> Except as otherwise provided by law, no recovery shall be had for any infringement committed more than six years prior to the filing of the complaint or counterclaim for infringement in the action.

The six-year damage period under 35 U.S.C. § 286 may be further reduced based on the patent marking rules in 35 U.S.C. § 287 (a), which state that:

> Patentees, and persons making, offering for sale, or selling within the United States any patented article for or under them, or importing any patented article into the United States, may give notice to the public that the same is patented, either by fixing thereon the word "patent" or the abbreviation "pat.", together with the number of the patent, or by fixing thereon the word "patent" or the abbreviation "pat." together with an address of a posting on the Internet, accessible to the public without charge for accessing the address, that associates the patented article with the number of the patent, or when, from the character of the article, this can not be done, by fixing to it, or to the package wherein one or more of them is contained, a label containing a like notice.

In the event of a failure to mark, 35 U.S.C. 287 (a) provides that:

> no damages shall be recovered by the patentee in any action for infringement, except on proof that the infringer was notified of the infringement and continued to infringe thereafter, in which event damages may be recovered only for infringement occurring after such notice. Filing of an action for infringement shall constitute such notice.

The impact of the patent marking laws on the damage period provided under 35 U.S.C. § 286 is complicated by additional factors beyond the scope of this book, including the type of patent claim asserted (i.e., method or apparatus).[9]

---

9. D.K. Mroz & L.M. Abu-Taleb, *Maximizing Damages: The Importance of Considering Marking Law When Selecting Claims to Assert in Litigation*, FINNEGAN (Sep./Oct. 2017).

Chapter 4

Choice Between Lost Profits and Reasonable Royalties

Chapter 3 addressed the current U.S. statutory law related to the quantification of monetary relief for patent infringement.

35 U.S.C. § 284 provides for the recovery of "damages adequate to compensate for infringement" but not less than a "reasonable royalty for the use made of the invention by the infringer." Therefore, reasonable royalties act as the floor for damages. Three outcomes arise from the preceding.

First, a patentee can recover its "damages adequate to compensate for infringement" using a lost profits methodology. Second, a patentee can recover damages using a reasonable royalty methodology if lost profits cannot be established. Third, a patentee can use a hybrid approach seeking lost profits on a portion of the infringing sales and reasonable royalties on the remaining.

This chapter addresses the choice between lost profits and reasonable royalty methodologies. Two tests used by the courts to establish entitlement to lost profits are (1) the Panduit Test and (2) the Two-Supplier Market Test.

Entitlement to Lost Profits

The recovery of lost profits requires the patentee to "prove a causal relationship between the infringement and its loss of profits."[1] According to

1. Crystal Semiconductor Corp. v. TriTech Microelectronics Int'l Inc. 246 F.3d 1326, 1354 (Fed. Cir. 2001) (citing BIC Leisure Prods., Inc. v. Windsurfing Int'l, Inc., 1 F.3d 1214, 1218 (Fed. Cir. 1993)).

the Federal Circuit, this requires a patentee to "show a reasonable probability that 'but for' the infringement, it would have made the sales that were made by the infringer."[2] The patentee must support the quantification of lost profits with "sound economic proof of the nature of the market and likely outcomes with infringement factored out of the picture."[3]

There is no required method for establishing but for causation.[4] Two tests used by the courts to establish entitlement to lost profits are (1) the Panduit Test and (2) the Two-Supplier Market Test.

The Panduit Test

Courts have accepted a "useful, but not exclusive" method for proving entitlement to lost profits, commonly known as the Panduit Test.[5]

The Panduit Test requires proof of (1) demand for the patented product, (2) absence of acceptable non-infringing substitutes, (3) the manufacturing and marketing capability to exploit demand, and (4) the amount of profit that the plaintiff would have made.[6] The preceding four factors are known as the Panduit Factors.

Panduit Factor No. 1: Demand

Panduit Factor No. 1 requires the patentee to prove that demand existed for the patented product.[7] The key phrase is "patented product." Panduit Factor No. 1 considers the demand for the product as a whole.[8]

---

2. Rite-Hite Corp. v. Kelley Co., Inc., 56 F.3d 1538, 1545 (Fed. Cir. 1995).
3. Compensatory Damages Issues in Patent Infringement Cases 3 (Fed. Judicial Ctr., 2d ed. 2017) (quoting Akamai Techs., Inc. v. Limelight Networks, Inc., 805 F.3d 1368, 1379 (Fed. Cir. 1993)).
4. Mentor Graphics Corp. v. EVE-USA, Inc., 851 F.3d 1275, 1284 (Fed Cir. 2017).
5. *Id.* (citing *Rite-Hite Corp.*, 56 F.3d at 1545) (citing Panduit Corp. v. Stahlin Bros Fibre Works, Inc., 575 F.2d 1152 (6th Cir. 1978)).
6. Panduit Corp. v. Stahlin Bros. Fibre Works, Inc., 575 F.2d 1152, 1156 (6th Cir. 1978).
7. *Id.*
8. Mentor Graphics Corp. v. Eve-USA, Inc., 851 F.3d 1275, 1285 (Fed. Cir. 2017) (citing DePuy Spine, Inc. v. Medtronic Sofamor Danek, Inc., 567 F.3d 1314, 1330–31 (Fed. Cir. 2009)).

As noted by the Federal Circuit in *DePuy Spine, Inc. v. Medtronic Sofamor Danek, Inc.*:[9]

> This factor does not require any allocation of consumer demand among the various limitations recited in a patent claim. Instead, the first Panduit Factor simply asks whether demand existed for the "patented product" i.e., a product that is "covered by the patent in suit" or that "directly competes with the infringing device."

Economic analyses and evidence that may assist with establishing demand for the patented product can be quantitative and qualitative. Quantitatively, a damages expert can, for example, analyze (1) historical unit and dollar sales of the patented and infringing products, (2) sales projections and budgets for the patented and infringing products, (3) sales backlog (i.e., unfulfilled orders), and (4) internal or external marketing reports or surveys related to consumer behavior and buying decisions. Qualitatively, a damages expert may consider other evidence indicating market demand. For example, when Apple released the iPhone 6, the media were inundated with stories of consumers waiting for hours in long lines to purchase their new phones. The preceding was echoed by millions of posts from individual consumers on social media.

Panduit Factor No. 2: Non-Infringing Substitutes

Panduit Factor No. 2 requires the patentee to prove the absence of non-infringing substitutes.[10] There is a relationship between Panduit Factor Nos. 1 and 2. While the first Panduit Factor considers "the demand for the patented product as a whole," the second considers the "demand for particular limitations or features of the claimed invention."[11] The satisfaction of Panduit Factor Nos. 1 and 2 "ties lost profit damages to specific

---

9. DePuy Spine, Inc. v. Medtronic Sofamor Danek, Inc., 567 F.3d 1314, 1330 (Fed. Cir. 2009).

10. Panduit Corp. v. Stahlin Bros. Fibre Works, Inc., 575 F.2d 1152, 1156 (6th Cir. 1978).

11. Mentor Graphics Corp. v. Eve-USA, Inc., 851 F.3d 1275, 1285 (Fed. Cir. 2017).

claim limitations and ensures that damages are commensurate with the value of the patented features."[12]

Proving Panduit No. 2, the absence of non-infringing substitutes, is often difficult.[13] A non-infringing substitute must have been acceptable and available.

What is an acceptable non-infringing substitute? As noted by the Federal Circuit in *Mentor Graphics Corp. v. Eve-USA, Inc.*:[14]

> if there is a noninfringing alternative which any given purchaser would have found acceptable and bought, then the patentee cannot obtain lost profits for that particular sale. For example, if the customer would have bought the infringing product without the patented feature or with a different, non-infringing alternative to the patented feature, then the patentee cannot establish entitlement to lost profits for that particular sale. And this determination is made on a customer-by-customer basis.

Price may also impact the acceptability of a non-infringing alternative. In an elastic market, the price of the alleged non-infringing alternative should not be markedly different from the patented product.[15]

What is an available non-infringing alternative? As noted by the Federal Circuit in *Grain Processing Corp. v. American Maize-Products Co.*:[16]

> The critical time period for determining availability of an alternative is the period of infringement for which the patent owner claims damages, i.e., the "accounting period."

12. *Id.*
13. *Id.* at 1286.
14. *Id.*
15. BIC Leisure Products, Inc. v. Windsurfing Int'l, Inc., 1 F.3d 1214, 1219 (Fed. Cir. 1993).
16. Grain Processing Corp. v. Am. Maize-Products Co. 185 F.3d 1341, 1353 (Fed. Cir. 1999).

The court may infer that a non-infringing substitute was not available if it was not on the market during the accounting period.[17] But as noted by the Federal Circuit in *Grain Processing Corp. v. American Maize-Products Co.*:[18]

> The accused infringer then has the burden to overcome this inference by showing that the substitute was available during the accounting period. Mere speculation or conclusory assertions will not suffice to overcome the inference. After all, the infringer chose to produce the infringing, rather than non-infringing, product. Thus, the trial court must proceed with caution in assessing proof of the availability of substitutes not actually sold during the period of infringement. Acceptable substitutes that the infringer proves were available during the accounting period can preclude or limit lost profits; substitutes only theoretically possible will not.

Panduit Factor No. 2 addresses a two-supplier and a multi-supplier market. In a two-supplier market, "the patent owner and infringer are the only suppliers in the market and the owner is seeking to recover profits lost through every sale made by the infringer."[19] In a multi-supplier market, the relevant market must be defined. As noted by the Federal Circuit in *Crystal Semiconductor Corp. v. Tritech Microelectronics International PTE Ltd.*:[20]

> To determine a patentee's market share, the record must accurately identify the market. This requires an analysis which excludes alternatives to the patented product with disparately different prices or significantly different characteristics.

---

17. *Id.*
18. *Id.*
19. State Indus., Inc. v. Mor-Flo Indus., Inc., 883 F.2d 1573, 1578 (Fed. Cir. 1989).
20. Crystal Semiconductor Corp. v. Tritech Microelectronics Int'l PTE Ltd., 246 F.3d 1336, 1356 (Fed. Cir. 2001).

The following illustration is an example of a two-supplier market.

Two-Supplier Market		
Market with Infringer		**Market without Infringer**
Infringer 40.0%		Patent Owner 100.0%
Patent Owner 60.0%		

In a two-supplier market, "it is reasonable to assume, provided the patent owner has the manufacturing and marketing capabilities, that it would have made the infringer's sales."[21]

In a two-supplier market, there are no non-infringing substitutes. However, a multi-supplier market may contain non-infringing substitutes. The existence of a non-infringing substitute does not preclude the recovery of lost profits. A patentee in a multi-supplier market with non-infringing substitutes can seek lost profits for a portion of the infringing sales based on its market share.[22]

A multi-supplier market includes (1) the patent owner, (2) the infringer, and (3) other competitors selling non-infringing substitutes. The following illustration is an example of a multi-supplier market.

21. State Indus., Inc. v. Mor-Flo Indus., Inc., 883 F.2d 1573, 1578 (Fed. Cir. 1989).
22. *Id.*

Two-Supplier Market		
Market with Infringer		**Market without Infringer**
Infringer 20.0%		Patent Owner 37.5%
Patent Owner 30.0%		
Non-Infringing Competitors 50.0%		Non-Infringing Competitors 62.5%

As noted in the preceding illustration, a market-share approach allocates the infringer's sales between the patent owner and the non-infringing competitors based on their market shares.

Establishing the lack of non-infringing substitutes may require the assistance of a technical expert, who can perform a comparison of the technical benefits of the patented technology versus other products in the market during the time of infringement. Additionally, other sources of information may help establish the lack of non-infringing substitutes.

Marketing studies performed or commissioned by the infringer may demonstrate the importance of the patented feature to consumers. Also, an analysis of the infringer's marketing material may be helpful. Advertisements, websites, and product information sheets may feature and demonstrate the patented feature. Third-party product reviews may highlight or explain the importance of the patented feature. Trade shows are another potential source of information. For example, many companies release new products at the Consumer Electronics Show. These product releases are often major events where the company's CEO highlights key features of the new product. Social media and internet search results may indicate consumer demand or excitement regarding the infringing feature.

Panduit Factor No. 3: Manufacturing and Marketing Capacity

Panduit Factor No. 3 requires the patentee to demonstrate that it had the manufacturing and marketing capacity to exploit the demand.[23]

A patent holder may demonstrate manufacturing capacity by establishing excess capacity or subcontracting. Excess capacity occurs when a manufacturer can increase production at its existing facilities. For example, a manufacturer may operate one eight-hour shift. So, the addition of additional shifts may have provided the excess capacity required to manufacture the infringing units. The feasibility of adding additional shifts may require input from company management and engineers. Additionally, the introduction of additional shifts may increase expenses, potentially leading to higher incremental costs. Absent excess capacity, a patent holder may demonstrate manufacturing capacity by establishing that a contract manufacturer could have manufactured the infringing units. A consideration when using a contract manufacturer is timing. The contract manufacturer may require set-up time and the logistics of shipping the product to the patent holder.

A patent holder must also demonstrate marketing capacity. The infringer and patent holder may sell through different channels. For example, the infringer may sell directly to the consumer while the patent holder sells to distributors. The infringer and patent holder may serve different geographic regions. For example, the infringer sells nationwide, while the patent holder sells only in the Northeast. Would the patent holder have the sales and distribution network to service customers nationwide? Regardless of the scenario, a patent holder must demonstrate that it could make the sale.

23. Panduit Corp. v. Stahlin Bros. Fibre Works, Inc., 575 F.2d 1152, 1156 (6th Cir. 1978).

Panduit Factor No. 4: Amount of Profit

Panduit Factor No. 4 requires the patentee to "prove the amount of profit he would have made."[24] Chapter 5 addresses the methodology and analyses used to quantify lost profits.

The Two-Supplier Market Test

The Two-Supplier Market Test predates the creation of the Federal Circuit.[25] To establish entitlement to lost profits under the Two-Supplier Market Test, a patentee must demonstrate (1) the existence of a two-supplier market, (2) the manufacturing and marketing capacity necessary to make the infringing sales, and (3) the amount of profit it would have made.[26]

As noted by the Federal Circuit in *Micro Chemical, Inc. v. Lextron*, the Two-Supplier Market Test "collapses the first two Panduit factors into one 'two suppliers in the relevant market' factor."[27]

24. *Id.*

25. K-Tec, Inc. v. Vita-Mix Corp., Case No. 2:06-CV-108-TC U.S. District Court, D. Utah, Central Division (Order and Memorandum, May 24, 2010).

26. Micro Chem., Inc. v. Lextron, Inc., 318 F.3d 1119, 1124 (Fed. Cir. 2003).

27. *Id.*

Chapter 5
Lost Profits Methodology

Chapter 4 addressed the entitlement to lost profits. This chapter addresses the quantification of damages using a lost profits methodology. Lost profits equals lost revenue less incremental expenses.

Lost revenue may arise from (1) infringing sales, (2) price erosion, and (3) convoyed or collateral sales. Determining lost profits requires deducting incremental costs. What are incremental costs? Answering this question begins with understanding fixed and variable cost behaviors as well as the concept of marginal cost. Identifying incremental costs may involve qualitative and quantitative analyses.

Lost Revenue

The determination of incremental lost profits begins with quantifying lost revenue.

Lost revenue may arise from one or more of the following: (1) infringing sales, (2) price erosion, and (3) convoyed or collateral sales.

Infringing Sales

In a two-supplier market, quantifying lost revenue requires financial information from the infringer and patent holder: (1) the number of infringing unit sales from the infringer and (2) the average selling price of the patented product from the patent holder. A multi-supplier market also requires the relative market shares of the infringer, the patent holder, and other companies selling non-infringing substitutes.

The following illustration quantifies lost revenue on infringing sales in a two-supplier market.

Lost Revenue: Infringing Units (Two-Supplier Market)								
		Damage Period						Total
		1	2	3	4	5	6	
Patented Product								
Revenue	[1]	$ 13,000	$ 14,000	$ 15,000	$ 16,000	$ 17,000	$ 18,000	$ 93,000
Units	[2]	6,500	7,000	7,500	8,000	8,500	9,000	46,500
ASP	[3]=[1]/[2]	$ 2.00	$ 2.00	$ 2.00	$ 2.00	$ 2.00	$ 2.00	$ 2.00
Infringing Units	[4]	10,000	12,000	14,000	15,000	16,000	17,000	84,000
Lost Revenue		**$20,000**	**$24,000**	**$28,000**	**$30,000**	**$32,000**	**$34,000**	**$168,000**

As indicated by the preceding illustration, the patent holder would have 100 percent of the market absent the infringer (i.e., they would make every infringing sale). The same is not true in a multi-supplier market. In a multi-supplier market with non-infringing substitutes, a patent holder can recover lost profits for the portion of its infringing sales attributable to its relative market share in the reconstructed market without the infringer.

The first step in quantifying lost revenue in a multi-supplier market is to reconstruct the market in the absence of the infringer.

The following illustration reconstructs the market without the infringer.

Reconstruction of Market without Infringer					
	Market with Infringer		Allocation of Infringer's Market Share		Market without Infringer
	[1]		[2]		[3]=[1]+[2]
Patent Holder	40.00%	[4]	17.1%	([4]/[8])*[9]	57.1%
Non-Infringing Competitor 1	10.00%	[5]	4.3%	([5]/[8])*[9]	14.3%
Non-Infringing Competitor 2	10.00%	[6]	4.3%	([6]/[8])*[9]	14.3%
Non-Infringing Competitor 3	10.00%	[7]	4.3%	([7]/[8])*[9]	14.3%
Non-Infringing Competitors	30.00%		12.9%		42.9%
Patent Holder & Non-Infringing Competitors	**70.00%**	[8]	**30.0%**		**100.0%**
Infringer	30.00%	[9]	-30.0%	-1*[9]	0.0%
Total Market	**100.00%**		**0.0%**		**100.0%**

As demonstrated in the following illustration, an infringer is entitled to lost profits on the infringer's sales based on its respective market share.

Lost Revenue: Infringing Units (Multi-Supplier Market)								
		Damage Period						
		1	**2**	**3**	**4**	**5**	**6**	**Total**
Patented Product								
Revenue	[1]	$ 13,000	$ 14,000	$ 15,000	$ 16,000	$ 17,000	$ 18,000	$ 93,000
Units	[2]	6,500	7,000	7,500	8,000	8,500	9,000	46,500
ASP	[3]=[1]/[2]	$ 2.00	$ 2.00	$ 2.00	$ 2.00	$ 2.00	$ 2.00	$ 2.00
Infringing Units	[4]	10,000	12,000	14,000	15,000	16,000	17,000	84,000
Market Share	[5]	57.1%	57.1%	57.1%	57.1%	57.1%	57.1%	57.1%
Lost Unit Sales	[6]=[4]*[5]	5,710	6,852	7,994	8,565	9,136	9,707	47,964
Lost Revenue	[7]=[6]*[3]	$ 11,420	$ 13,704	$ 15,988	$ 17,130	$ 18,272	$ 19,414	$ 95,928

In a two-supplier market, the patent holder received lost profits on 100 percent of the 84,000 infringing unit sales. In the multi-supplier market, the patent holder received lost profits on 57.1 percent of the 84,000 units, that is, 47,964. The non-infringing competitors would have made the remaining 36,036 unit sales. However, the patent holder would be entitled to a reasonable royalty on the 36,036 unit sales.

Price Erosion

As noted by the Federal Circuit in *Power Integrations, Inc. v. Fairchild Semiconductor International, Inc.*, "damages for infringement may account for both lost sales and reduction of prices due to infringing competition."[1]

In 1886, the Supreme Court opened the door for price erosion in *Yale Lock Manufacturing Co. v. Sargent*, stating that the "[R]eduction of prices and consequent loss of profits, enforced by infringing competition, is a proper ground for awarding damages."[2] The Supreme Court said,

1. Power Integrations, Inc. v. Fairchild Semiconductor Int'l, Inc., 711 F.3d 1348, 1378 (Fed. Cir. 1984).
2. Yale Lock Mfg. Co. v. Sargent, 117 U.S. 536, 551 (1886).

"[T]he only question is as to the character and sufficiency of the evidence in the particular case."[3]

As noted by the Federal Circuit in *Crystal Semiconductor Corp. v. Tritech Microelectronics International, Inc.*, the preceding question "places the burden on the patentee to show that 'but for' infringement, it would have sold its products at higher prices."[4] So, "in a credible economic analysis, the patentee cannot show entitlement to a higher price divorced from the effect of that higher price on demand for the product."[5]

The economic law of demand addresses the relationship between price and quantity demanded. It states that as the price of a given commodity increases, the quantity demanded decreases, all else equal.

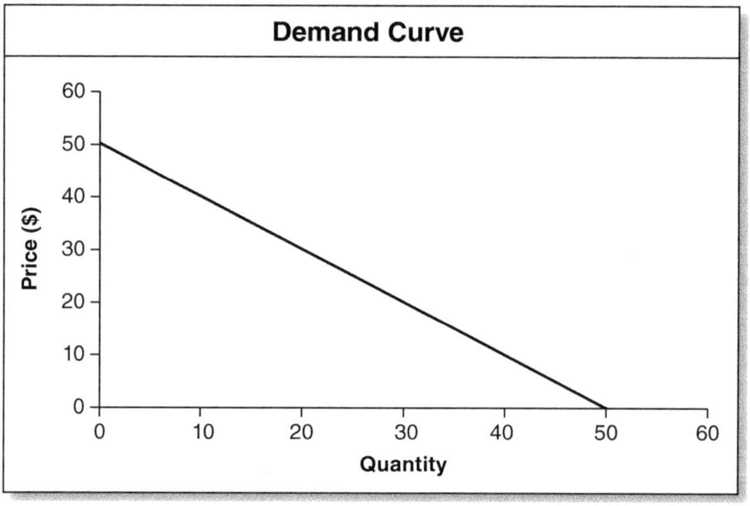

As illustrated here, the demand curve is downward sloping: As price increases, quantity demanded decreases. The price elasticity of demand is:[6]

3. *Id.*

4. Crystal Semiconductor Corp. v. Tritech Microelectronics Int'l, Inc., 246 F.3d 1336, 1357 (Fed. Cir. 2001).

5. *Id.*

6. G.W. Mankiw, Principles of Microeconomics 90 (Carnegie Learning 2018).

a measure of how much the quantity demanded of a good responds to a change in the price of that good computed as the percentage change in quantity demanded divided by the percentage of change in price.

Demand may be elastic if the quantity demanded responds significantly to changes in price, or inelastic if it responds minimally.[7] The price elasticity of demand is related to the slope of the demand curve.[8] So, the steeper the demand curve, the less impact a price change has on the quantity demanded. The flatter the demand curve, the greater impact a price change has on the quantity demanded.

Three approaches used to establish price erosion include (1) the direct comparison approach, (2) the before-and-after approach, and (3) the benchmark approach. The direct comparison approach uses direct evidence of price reductions from head-to-head competition between the patent holder and the infringer. The direct comparison approach takes a macro perspective and compares the patent holder's prices pre- and post-infringement. The benchmark approach uses the prices of other products unaffected by the infringement to quantify price erosion.

Convoyed Sales

A convoyed sale "is a sale of a product that is not patented, but is sufficiently related to the patented product such that the patentee may recover lost profits for lost sales."[9]

Two conditions must be met to recover lost profits on convoyed sales. First, there must be a functional relationship with the patented product.[10] Selling convoyed and infringing products together for "convenience or business advantage" does not constitute a functional relationship.[11] Further, if "the convoyed sale has a use independent of the patented device, that suggests a non-functional relationship."[12] Second, the losses from

---

7. *Id.*
8. *Id.* at 93.
9. Warsaw Orthopedic, Inc. v. NuVasive, Inc., 778 F.3d 1365, 1375 (Fed. Cir. 2015).
10. *Id.*
11. *Id.*
12. *Id.*

selling convoyed products must be reasonable and foreseeable.[13] Like lost profits, damages for convoyed sales are recoverable if the patent holder establishes that it would have made the sales but for the infringement.

Incremental Costs

Lost profits are quantified on an incremental basis, that is, lost profits equals lost revenue less incremental expenses.

As noted by the Federal Circuit in *Paper Converting Machine Co. v. Magna-Graphics Corp.*, the incremental profit approach:[14]

> recognizes that it does not cost as much to produce unit N+1 in the first N (or fewer) units produced already have paid the fixed costs. Thus fixed costs—those which do not vary with increases in production, such as management salaries, property taxes, and insurance—are excluded when determining profits.

Understanding incremental profits begins with considering cost behaviors. Cost behavior describes how costs change in response to changes in output. There are two types of cost behavior: variable and fixed. These cost behaviors provide the foundation for understanding the related concepts of marginal and incremental costs.

Variable and Fixed Cost Behaviors

A variable cost changes in proportion to changes in sales, while a fixed cost remains constant for a period, regardless of changes in sales. To illustrate these cost behaviors, consider a pizza shop. Variable costs would include the dough, cheese, sauce, and toppings. These costs are incurred every time a pizza is made. In other words, the costs of the dough, cheese, sauce, and toppings move in proportion with the number of pizzas made. A fixed cost of a pizza shop would be the cost to purchase the pizza oven.

---

13. *Id.*

14. Paper Converting Mach. Co. v. Magna-Graphics Corp., 745 F.2d 11, 22 (Fed. Cir. 1984).

This cost remains unchanged in total for a specific time period regardless of the number of pizzas sold.

The following illustration provides a graphical depiction of variable and fixed costs.

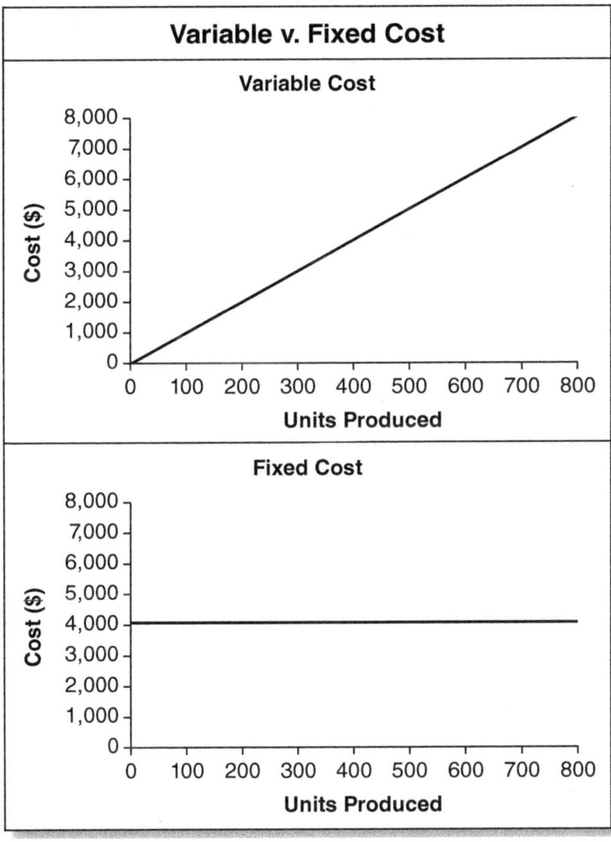

Costs are variable or fixed for a specific time period and activity. For example, the oven at the pizza shop has a capacity of 1,500 pizzas per day. So, if the pizza shop sells more than 1,500 pizzas a day, an additional oven will be required. This type of cost behavior is also known as a step cost. Step costs remain fixed for a given level of output and increase or decrease once a certain threshold is reached.

The following is a graphical illustration of a step cost.

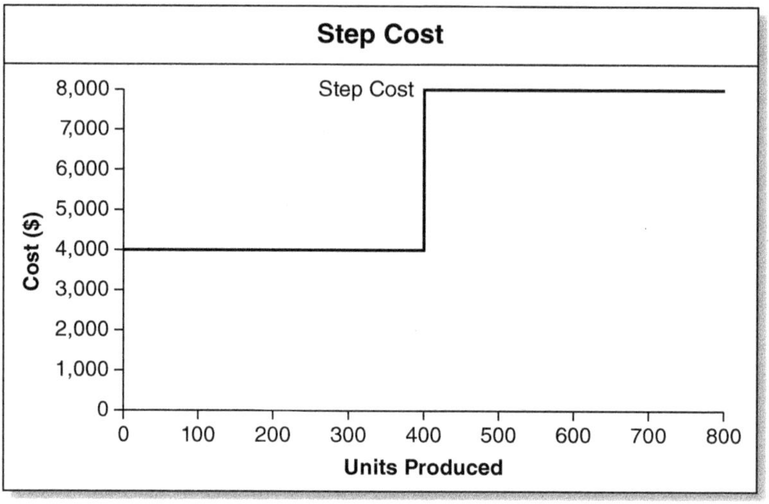

Relationship Between Marginal and Incremental Costs

Marginal cost is "the increase in total cost that arises from an extra unit of production,"[15] whereas incremental cost is the increase in total cost that arises over a specific increment of production. In the context of lost profits, incremental costs are those incurred to make and sell the infringing units.

Identification of Incremental Costs

Identifying incremental costs may involve qualitative and quantitative analyses. The starting point for either analysis is identifying the costs associated with the infringing sales. This often begins with an income statement.

An income statement, also called a profit and loss statement, shows "how much money a company made and spent over a specific period of time (such as over the company's fiscal year)."[16] The income statement

15. Mankiw, *supra* note 6, at 256.

16. SEC, Office of the Advocate for Small Business Capital Formation, Glossary.

includes (1) revenue, which "is the dollar value of all the products an entity sold or services it provided to its customers," and (2) expenses, which are "something spent on a specific item for a particular purpose."[17]

The following illustration summarizes Apple Inc.'s historical income statements.[18]

Apple, Inc. Historical Income Statements			
	Fiscal Year Ended		
(millions)	**2022**	**2023**	**2024**
Revenue	$ 394,328	$ 383,285	$ 391,035
COGS	$ 223,546	$ 214,137	$ 210,352
Gross Profit	$ 170,782	$ 169,148	$ 180,683
Operating Expenses			
SG&A	$ 25,094	$ 24,932	$ 26,097
R&D	$ 26,251	$ 29,915	$ 31,370
	$ 51,345	$ 54,847	$ 57,467
Operating Profit	$ 119,437	$ 114,301	$ 123,216

The preceding illustration identifies three major expenses: (1) COGS (i.e., cost of goods sold), (2) SG&A (i.e., selling, general, and administrative), and (3) Research and Development (R&D). COGS refers to the costs associated with producing finished goods and services. SG&A includes other costs of running the business that are not directly related to producing finished goods. Research and Development are the costs incurred to develop new products or improve existing ones.

COGS, SG&A, and R&D are individually comprised of numerous expenses. A crucial step in identifying incremental costs is understanding the composition of these expense categories, which may be accomplished through interviews with management, deposition testimony, or analysis of underlying financial records such as trial balances or general ledgers.

COGS may include materials, direct labor, packaging, and manufacturing overhead. Typically, COGS is a largely variable cost. But it may include fixed costs, such as supervisory salaries, which do not vary with

17. *Id.* and New York State Society of CPAs Accounting Terminology Guide.
18. SEC Form 10-K, Apple Inc. for the fiscal year ended September 28, 2024.

the incremental sales in question. SG&A may include expenses for sales commissions, management salaries, advertising, marketing, rent, professional fees, and travel, among others. SG&A may consist of both fixed and variable costs. For example, commissions based on sales may be variable, while rent is fixed and unlikely to vary with sales. R&D may include salaries, research materials, and laboratory fees, among others. R&D is typically a fixed cost based on annual budgets set by management.

Quantitative analysis can also help identify incremental costs. The following illustration summarizes the components of the COGS related to infringing sales.

Infringing Sales & COGS						
	Year					
	1	**2**	**3**	**4**	**5**	**6**
Infringing Units	100	200	300	400	500	600
ASP	$ 1,000	$ 1,000	$ 1,000	$ 1,000	$ 1,000	$ 1,000
Infringing Sales	$ 100,000	$ 200,000	$ 300,000	$ 400,000	$ 500,000	$ 600,000
COGS						
Materials	$ 25,000	$ 50,000	$ 75,000	$ 100,000	$ 125,000	$ 150,000
Manufacturing Labor	$ 20,000	$ 40,000	$ 60,000	$ 80,000	$ 100,000	$ 120,000
Supervisory Labor	$ 30,000	$ 30,000	$ 30,000	$ 30,000	$ 30,000	$ 30,000
Total COGS	$ 75,000	$ 120,000	$ 165,000	$ 210,000	$ 255,000	$ 300,000

In the preceding simplified illustration, it is evident that supervisory labor is a fixed cost, that is, it does not vary with the increases in infringing units. However, it is not apparent when looking at total COGS, underscoring the importance of understanding and analyzing individual expenses (i.e., materials, manufacturing labor, and supervisory labor).

A scatter diagram provides another tool that helps identify incremental costs. It looks for a relationship, or correlation, between two variables plotted on each axis. The following illustration plots the materials, manufacturing labor, and supervisory labor on the y-axis and the infringing units on the x-axis.

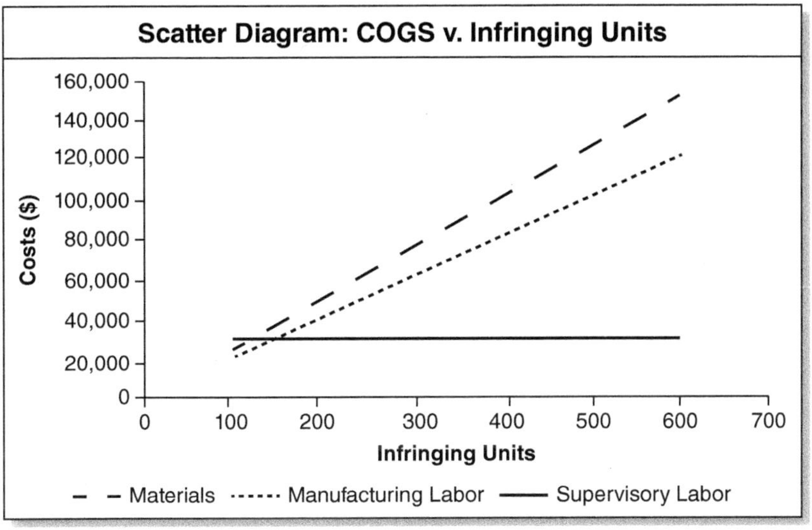

The preceding graphically illustrates that materials and manufacturing costs are incremental (i.e., they vary with the number of infringing units). At the same time, supervisory labor is fixed (i.e., it remains constant regardless of the number of infringing units).

Chapter 6
Reasonable Royalty Methodology

Per 35 U.S.C. § 284, a reasonable royalty sets the floor for damages "adequate to compensate for the infringement." Determining a reasonable royalty shares similarities with a fair market valuation of a patent using the Cost, Market, and Income Approaches. The premise of the Cost Approach is that a prudent investor would pay no more for an asset than its replacement or reproduction cost. The Income Approach establishes value based on a portion of the present value of the future economic benefits that accrue to the licensee. The Market Approach establishes value through an analysis of comparable transactions.

Three approaches used by the courts to quantify a reasonable royalty are (1) the established royalty, (2) hypothetical negotiation (aka willing licensor/willing licensee approach), and (3) the analytical method.

Established Royalty

A reasonable royalty may be based on an "established royalty."[1] As noted by the Federal Circuit, "[W]here an established royalty rate for the patented inventions is shown to exist, the rate will usually be adopted as the best measure of reasonable and entire compensation."[2]

An established royalty "must be paid by such a number of persons as to indicate a general acquiescence in its reasonableness by those who have occasion to use the invention."[3] In addition, "[A] single licensing agreement, without more, is insufficient proof of an established royalty."[4]

1. Hanson v. Alpine Ski Area, Inc., 718 F.2d 1075, 1078 (Fed. Cir. 1983).
2. *Id.* (quoting Tektronix, Inc. v. United States, 552 F.2d. 343, 347 (Ct. Cl. 1977)).
3. *Id.* at 1078 (quoting Rude v. Westcott, 130 U.S. 152, 165 (S. Ct. 1889)).
4. Trell v. Marlee Elec. Corp., 912 F.2d 1443, 1446 (Fed. Cir. 1990).

In limited circumstances, a reasonable royalty may exceed the established royalty. As noted by the Federal Circuit, "a royalty 'reasonable under 35 U.S.C. § 284 may be greater than an established royalty."[5] This could occur when "the evidence clearly shows that widespread infringement made the established royalty artificially low."[6]

Hypothetical Negotiation

The hypothetical negotiation "attempts to ascertain the royalty upon which the parties would have agreed had they successfully negotiated an agreement just before infringement began."[7] It attempts to "recreate the *ex ante* licensing negotiation scenario and to describe the resulting agreement."[8] The question addressed in the hypothetical negotiation is "if on the eve of infringement, a willing licensor and a licensee had entered into an agreement instead of allowing infringement of the patent to take place, what would that agreement be?"[9]

The hypothetical negotiation assumes that (1) the asserted patent is valid and infringed, and (2) it involved a willing licensor and willing licensee. As noted by the Federal Circuit in *Tektronix, Inc. v. The United States*:[10]

> [T]he willing buyer/willing-seller concept is, as Judge Learned Hand termed it, "a device in aid of justice." As such it is employed by the court as a means of arriving at reasonable compensation and its validity does not depend on the actual willingness of the parties to the lawsuit to engage in such negotiations.

The determination of a reasonable royalty "must relate to the time infringement occurred, and not be an after-the-fact assessment."[11] In fact, "the key element in setting a reasonable royalty is the necessity for return

---

5. Nickson Indus., Inc. v. Rol Mfg., Ltd., 847 F.2d 795, 798 (Fed. Cir. 1988).
6. *Id.*
7. Lucent Technologies, Inc. v. Gateway, Inc., 580 F.3d 1301, 1324.
8. *Id.* at 1325.
9. LaserDynamics, Inv. v. Quanta Comput., Inc., 694 F.3d 51, 76 (Fed. Cir. 2012).
10. Tektronix, Inc. v. The United States, 552 F.2d 343, 349 (U.S. Court of Claims 1977).
11. 694 F.3d at 75.

to the date when the infringement began."[12] The preceding is consistent with generally accepted valuation methodology, where the conclusion of value is based on the information that was known or knowable as of the valuation date.

However, courts may allow the use of evidence from after the date of hypothetical negotiation based on the "book of wisdom," which originates from *Sinclair Refining Co. v. Jenkins Petroleum Process Co.*[13]

This case noted that:[14]

> a different situation is presented if years have gone by before the evidence is offered. Experience is then available to correct uncertain prophecy. Here is a book of wisdom that courts may not neglect. We find no rule of law that sets a clasp upon its pages, and forbids us to look within.

Consistent with valuation theory, a key consideration is whether the post-hypothetical negotiation facts were known or knowable. As noted in *Probatter Sports, LLC v. Sports Tutor, Inc.*:[15,16]

> The Court concludes that post-hypothetical negotiation facts and circumstances are only relevant when facts known at the time of the hypothetical negotiation were predictive of future facts and events which later materialized. Such predictive facts are ones which the hypothetical negotiators could have rationally projected based on then-known facts. In other words, the book of wisdom does not authorize rank speculation; but authorizes instead consideration of facts the hypothetical negotiators could have known at the time of the hypothetical negotiation, as well as facts and events they could have reasonably inferred or extrapolated from the known facts. Finally, future events may enlighten the court as to the facts known at the time of the hypothetical negotiation and the weight the negotiators may have given those facts.

---

12. *Id.* (citing Hanson v. Alpine Valley Ski Area, Inc., 718 F.2d 1075, 1079 (Fed. Cir. 1983)).
13. Sinclair Refining Co. v. Jenkins Petroleum Process Co., 289 U.S. 689 (S. Ct. 1933).
14. *Id.* at 698.
15. Probatter Sports, LLC v. Sports Tutor, Inc., 586 F.3d 80, 92 (2022).
16. *Id.* at 90–92 provides a good history of the book of wisdom.

Georgia-Pacific *Factors*

The Federal Circuit sanctioned the use of the factors identified in *Georgia-Pacific Corp. v. United States Plywood* to frame a reasonable royalty inquiry (Georgia-Pacific Factors).[17,18] According to the Federal Circuit, the Georgia-Pacific Factors "properly tie the reasonable royalty calculation to the facts of the hypothetical negotiation at issue."[19]

The Federal Circuit also recognized that the Georgia-Pacific Factors were not a formula for quantifying a reasonable royalty, stating:[20]

> [T]here is no formula by which these factors can be rated precisely in the order of their relative importance or by which their economic significance can be automatically transduced into their pecuniary equivalent.

Instead, the Georgia-Pacific Factors provide a framework for the types of information considered in an expert's reasonable royalty analysis.

The court based the Georgia-Pacific Factors on a survey of leading cases.[21] There are 15 Georgia-Pacific Factors.

The following illustration categorizes the Georgia-Pacific Factors based on the financial and economic elements they address.

Classification of Georgia-Pacific Factors	
Category	**Georgia-Pacific Factors**
Market Comparable Royalties	1, 2, and 12
Licensing Policies, Terms, and Relationships	3, 4, 5, and 7
Advantages and Benefits of Patented Technology	9 and 10
Profitability and Benefits of Patent	6, 8, 11, and 13
Opinions of Qualified Experts	14
Hypothetical Negotiation	15

17. Uniloc USA, Inc. v. Microsoft Corp., 632 F.3d 1292, 1317 (Fed. Cir. 2011).
18. See Appendix 2 for unabridged Georgia-Pacific Factors.
19. Uniloc USA, Inc. v. Microsoft Corp., 632 F.3d 1292, 1317 (Fed. Cir. 2011).
20. Georgia-Pacific Corp. v. U.S. Plywood Corp., 318 F. Supp. 1116, 1120–21 (1970).
21. *Id.* at 1120.

An analysis of Georgia-Pacific Factors 1 to 14 provides the basis for the agreed-upon reasonable royalty resulting from the hypothetical negotiation (Factor 15) between a willing licensee and a willing licensor.

Market Comparable Royalties (Factors 1, 2, and 12)

Georgia-Pacific Factors 1, 2, and 12 address licensing transactions, if any, entered into by a plaintiff, defendant, or third party that involve, or are comparable to, the subject patent. Established or comparable royalties may provide evidence of the result of a hypothetical license involving the subject patent.

Georgia-Pacific Factor 1 addresses:[22]

> The royalties received by the patentee for the licensing of the patent in suit, proving or tending to prove an established royalty.

Georgia-Pacific Factor 2 addresses:[23]

> The rates paid by the licensee for the use of other patents comparable to the patent in suit.

Georgia-Pacific Factor 12 addresses:[24]

> The portion of the profit or of the selling price that may be customary in the particular business or in comparable businesses to allow for the use of the invention or analogous inventions.

Factors 1, 2, and 12 address comparable royalty rates. Comparison is "an examination of two or more items to establish similarities or dissimilarities."[25] As noted by the Federal Circuit in *Laserdynamics, Inc. v. Quanta Computer USA, Inc.*:[26]

22. *Id.*
23. *Id.*
24. *Id.*
25. Merriam Webster Dictionary.
26. Laserdynamics, Inc. v. Quanta Comput., Inc., 694 F.3d 51, 79 (Fed. Cir. 2012).

When relying on licenses to prove a reasonable royalty, alleging a loose or vague comparability between different technologies or licenses does not suffice.

On numerous occasions, the Federal Circuit determined that "a patentee could not rely on license agreements that were 'radically different from the hypothetical agreement under consideration.'"[27]

The "technological and economic differences" between license agreements must be considered when assessing comparability.[28] Some of these differences may arise from (1) timing (i.e., before or after the hypothetical negotiation), (2) nature of technology, (3) additional rights conferred in the agreement (e.g., use of trademarks), (4) the duration of the license, and (5) scope and restrictions.

Another potential comparability issue is the use of license agreements negotiated in anticipation of or as part of litigation proceedings. The courts have a "longstanding disapproval of relying on settlement agreements to establish reasonable royalty damages."[29] However, under limited circumstances, the courts have permitted the use of settlement agreements to establish a reasonable royalty.[30] In these limited circumstances, the courts must "consider the license in its proper context within the hypothetical negotiation framework to ensure that the reasonable royalty rate reflects 'the economic demand for the claimed technology.'"[31]

Licensing Policies, Terms, and Relationships (Factors 3, 4, 5, and 7)

Georgia-Pacific Factors 3, 4, 5, and 7 consider the nature and scope of a license resulting from the hypothetical negotiation and the impact of the parties' commercial relationship and past licensing policies on the reasonable royalty.

---

27. Uniloc USA, Inc. v. Microsoft Corp., 632 F.3d 1292, 1316 (Fed. Cir. 2011).
28. Resqnet.com, Inc. v. Kaplan & Gilman, LLP, 594 F.3d 860, 873 (Fed. Cir. 2010).
29. Laserdynamics, Inc. v. Quanta Comput., Inc., 694 F.3d 51, 77 (Fed. Cir. 2012).
30. *Id.*
31. *Id.*

Georgia-Pacific Factor 3 addresses:[32]

> The nature and scope of the license, as exclusive or non-exclusive; or as restricted or non-restricted in terms of territory or with respect to whom the manufactured product may be sold.

Exclusivity allows the licensee to realize the full economic benefit as the sole licensee of the patented technology. Conversely, exclusivity prevents the licensor from granting additional licenses to generate income, making the licensee the sole source of income. As a result, a licensor will demand, and a licensee will pay, a higher royalty rate for an exclusive license than a non-exclusive license. Likewise, a licensee will generally pay a higher royalty rate for a non-restricted license than for a restricted license.

Georgia-Pacific Factor 4 addresses:[33]

> The licensor's established policy and marketing program to maintain his patent monopoly by not licensing others to use the invention or by granting licenses under special conditions designed to preserve that monopoly.

A higher royalty rate may be justified when a licensor maintains the value of its patent through an established policy of not granting license agreements. Conversely, a lower royalty rate may be justified when a licensor actively licenses its patent, which may erode a licensee's advantages due to increased competition.

Georgia-Pacific Factor 5 addresses:[34]

> The commercial relationship between the licensor and licensee, such as, whether they are competitors in the same territory in the same line of business; or whether they are inventor and promotor.

---

32. Georgia-Pacific Corp. v. U.S. Plywood Corp., 318 F. Supp. 1116, 1120 (1970).
33. *Id.*
34. *Id.*

Generally, a licensor demands a higher royalty when the licensee is a direct competitor. In effect, the licensor demands a higher royalty to offset potential lost sales due to direct competition from the licensee. Conversely, a licensor may accept a lower royalty when the licensee is not a direct competitor. Consider, for example, a licensor that does not practice the patent and generates revenue solely from licensing.

Georgia-Pacific Factor 7 addresses:[35]

> The duration of the patent and the term of the license.

The impact of patent life and license term on a reasonable royalty is dependent on the facts and circumstances. Sometimes, the remaining term of a patent has an upward impact on the royalty rate. For example, a long patent term allows the licensor to recover its investment in the accused product. Also, absent a license, a patent may prevent the licensor from entering the market. The longer the licensor is out of the market, the greater the economic costs. Other times, the remaining term of a patent has a downward impact on the royalty rate. This generally occurs in industries where the technology's life cycle is shorter than the remaining term of the patent.

Advantages and Benefits of Patented Technology (Factors 9 and 10)

Georgia-Pacific Factors 9 and 10 address the advantages and benefits of the patented technology.

Georgia-Pacific-Factor 9 addresses:[36]

> The utility and advantages of the patent property over the old modes or devices, if any, that had been used for working out similar results.

Generally, the cost of switching to a non-infringing technology sets the ceiling of a licensing negotiation. All things equal, a licensee will not pay a royalty that exceeds the cost of (1) obtaining a non-infringing substitute or (2) designing around the patent in question. The reasonable

35. *Id.*
36. *Id.*

royalty rate may increase if switching costs are high and decrease if they are low.

Georgia-Pacific Factor 10 addresses:[37]

> The nature of the patented invention; the character of the commercial embodiment of it as owned and produced by the licensor; and the benefits to those who have used the invention.

The importance of the patented technology to a product's commercial success can impact the magnitude of a reasonable royalty. Generally, a licensor will pay a higher or lower royalty depending on the patented features' contribution to the accused product's overall success.

Profitability and Benefits of Patent (Factors 6, 8, 11, and 13)

Georgia-Pacific Factors 6, 8, 11, and 13 address the profitability and benefits of the patent in suit.

Georgia-Pacific Factor 6 addresses:[38]

> The effect of selling the patented specialty in promoting sales of other products of the licensee; the existing value of the invention to the licensor as a generator of sales of his non-patented items; and the extent of such derivative or convoyed sales.

Convoyed sales represent:[39]

> The sale of unpatented collateral products that are functionally or economically related to the sale of an infringing product.

Typically, the existence of convoyed and derivative sales has an upward impact on a reasonable royalty rate. Generally, the level and the importance of collateral sales to the business affect the magnitude of the increase in the reasonable royalty rate.

---

37. *Id.*

38. *Id.*

39. Black's Law Dictionary 1604 (11th ed.).

Georgia-Pacific Factor 8 addresses:[40]

> The established profitability of the product made under the patent; its commercial success; and its current popularity.

The commercial success and the expected profitability of the patented product on the hypothetical negotiation date are factors that may directly impact the selection of a reasonable royalty. All things equal, a licensee may be willing to pay a higher royalty for an established, successful, and profitable patented product.

Georgia-Pacific Factor 11 addresses:[41]

> The extent to which the infringer has made use of the invention, and any evidence probative of the value of that use.

The nature and extent of an infringer's use of the patented technology and the corresponding value may impact the selection of a reasonable royalty. For example, a higher royalty rate may be justified when an infringer regularly uses the patented technology to generate value.

Georgia-Pacific Factor 13 addresses:[42]

> The portion of the realizable profit that should be credited to the invention as distinguished from non-patented elements, the manufacturing process, business risks, or significant features or improvements added by the infringer.

A variety of assets may contribute to a product's overall profitability. Consider, for example, a multi-component product covered by multiple patents. In this example, the infringing patent is one of several patents required to sell a product. In a hypothetical negotiation, the parties consider the portion of total profits attributable to the infringed patent. Typically, the larger the profits attributable to the infringed patent, the higher the royalty.

---

40. Georgia-Pacific Corp. v. U.S. Plywood Corp., 318 F. Supp. 1116, 1120 (1970).

41. *Id.*

42. *Id.*

Opinions of Qualified Experts

Georgia-Pacific Factor 14 addresses:[43]

> The opinion testimony of qualified experts.

The damages expert may rely on other non-economic experts. For example, a technical expert may provide useful information on the advantages, the technical feasibility of designing around the patent-in-suit, or the identification of non-infringing alternatives.

Hypothetical Negotiation

Georgia-Pacific Factor 15 addresses:[44]

> The amount that a licensor (such as the patentee) and a licensee (such as the infringer) would have agreed upon (at the time the infringement began) if both had been reasonably and voluntarily trying to reach an agreement; that is, the amount which a prudent licensee—who desired, as a business proposition, to obtain a license to manufacture and sell a particular article embodying the patented invention—would have been willing to pay as a royalty and yet be able to make a reasonable profit and which amount would have been acceptable by a prudent patentee who was willing to grant a license.

This factor is the culmination of an analysis of Georgia-Pacific Factors 1–14 and answers the question: "If, on the eve of infringement, a willing licensor and a licensee had entered into an agreement instead of allowing infringement of the patent to take place, what would that agreement be?"[45]

The hypothetical negotiation assumes that (1) the asserted patent is valid and infringed, and (2) it involved a willing licensor and willing licensee. These conditions may differ from a real-world negotiation. Unlike the hypothetical negotiation, parties in a real-world negotiation would consider the economic impact of validity and infringement, that is,

---

43. *Id.*

44. *Id.*

45. LaserDynamics, Inv. V. Quanta Comput., Inc., 694 F.3d 51, 76 (Fed. Cir. 2012).

the risk that the patent would be invalidated or that the potential licensee's use of the patent in question would not infringe. Additionally, in the real world, a licensor that competes with a potential licensee would not be willing to enter into a license agreement.

Analytical Method

The analytical method is another approach for quantifying a reasonable royalty. Addressed by the circuit court in *TWM Mfg. v. Dura Corp.*, the analytical method determines a reasonable royalty by "subtracting the infringer's usual or acceptable net profit from its anticipated net profit realized from sales of infringing devices."[46]

The analytical method attempts to isolate the excess profit attributable to the patented invention and provide a portion of those excess profits to the patent owner in the form of a royalty. The analytical method requires (1) an analysis of the infringer's expected or projected profits at the time of infringement, and (2) a determination of the benchmark earnings retained by the infringer before the allocation of any excess profits to the patent owner (i.e., economic contribution of the patented technology).

The following illustrates the isolation of the economic contribution of the patented feature.

Analytical Economic Contribution of Parented Feature

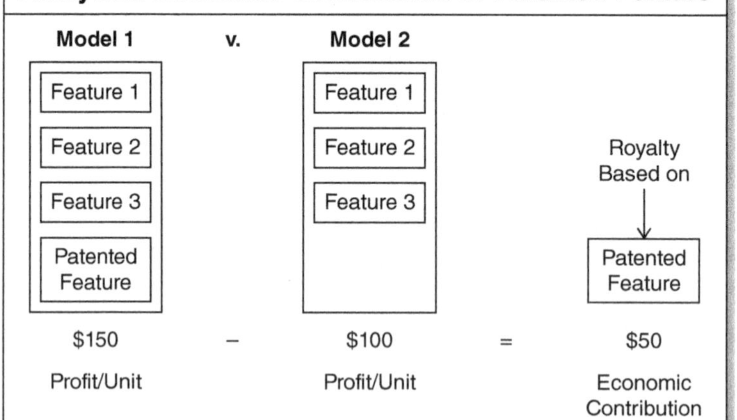

46. TWM Mfg. Co., Inc. v. Dura Corp., 789 F.2.d, 895, 899 (Fed. Cir. 1986).

Model 1 represents the infringing product, which includes four features, including the patented feature. The infringer also sells Model 2, which does not include the patented feature, but is otherwise identical to Model 1. Therefore, the difference in the profit/unit between Model 1 and Model 2 represents the economic contribution of the patented feature.

The final step of the analytical method is to allocate the economic contribution of the patented feature between the infringer and the patent holder. In other words, how much of the economic contribution would the infringer be willing to give up, and what would the patent holder accept for use of the patented technology?

The following illustration sets out the quantification of a reasonable royalty using the analytical method.

Analytical Method: Calculation of Damages

	Year					
	1	**2**	**3**	**4**	**5**	**6**
Profit/Unit						
Model 1 (with Infringing Feature)	$ 150	$ 150	$ 150	$ 150	$ 150	$ 150
Model 2 (without Infringing Feature)	$ 100	$ 100	$ 100	$ 100	$ 100	$ 100
Profit/Unit (Infringing Feature)	$ 50	$ 50	$ 50	$ 50	$ 50	$ 50
Profit Split	50%	50%	50%	50%	50%	50%
Reasonable Royalty	$ 25	$ 25	$ 25	$ 25	$ 25	$ 25
Infringing Units	5,000	8,000	9,000	12,000	13,000	15,000
Reasonable Royalties	$ 125,000	$ 200,000	$ 225,000	$ 300,000	$ 325,000	$ 375,000
Total Damages						$ 1,550,000

Chapter 7
Defendant's Profits Methodology

35 U.S.C. § 289 provides an additional remedy for the infringement of a design patent in the form of the defendant's profits.

The determination of the defendant's profits begins with the quantification of the revenue from the product covered by the design patent. Similar to the lost profits methodology, the determination of the defendant's profits requires deducting the related incremental costs. Chapter 5 addressed the concept of incremental costs, which are equally applicable to the defendant's profit methodology.

35 U.S.C. § 289 states (emphasis added) that

> Whoever during the term of a patent for a design, without license of the owner, (1) applies the patented design, or any colorable imitation thereof, to any **article of manufacture** for the purpose of sale, or (2) sells or exposes for sale any **article of manufacture** to which such design or colorable imitation has been applied shall be liable to the owner to the extent of his **total profit**, but not less than $250, recoverable in any United States district court having jurisdiction of the parties.

The quantification of the defendant's profits under 35 U.S.C. § 289 is a two-step process: (1) identification of the "article of manufacture" to which the infringed design was applied, and (2) calculating the "total profit" earned on that "article of manufacture."[1]

The Supreme Court addressed the term "article of manufacture" in *Samsung Electronics Co., Ltd. v. Apple Inc.*[2] The case involved design patents owned by Apple covering a smartphone with a rectangular front face,

1. Samsung Electronics Co., Ltd. v. Apple Inc., 137 S. Ct. 429, 434 (2016).
2. *Id.* at 429.

rounded edges, and a grid of colored icons on a screen.[3] The jury found that Samsung infringed Apple's design patents and awarded $399 million in monetary relief, which represented Samsung's total profit from the sale of infringing phones.[4] Samsung appealed on the basis that profits should have been limited "because the relevant articles of manufacture were the front face or screen rather than the entire smartphone."[5] The Federal Circuit rejected Samsung's argument and affirmed Apple's award of monetary relief.[6] The Supreme Court thus addressed whether "article of manufacture" was broad enough to cover the entire product and a component of that product.[7]

The Supreme Court held that:[8]

> In the case of a multicomponent product, the relevant "article of manufacture" for arriving at a § 289 damages award need not be the end product sold to the consumer but may be only a component of that product.

The Supreme Court did not "set out a test for identifying the relevant article of manufacture at the first step of the § 289 damages inquiry[.]"[9]

However, the Supreme Court did recognize the challenge with identifying the "article of manufacture" for a multi-component product, stating:[10]

> In the case of a design for a single-component product, such as a dinner plate, the product is the "article of manufacture." In the case of a design for a multicomponent product, such as a kitchen oven, identifying the "article of manufacture" to which the design has been applied is a more difficult task.

---

3. *Id.* at 431.
4. *Id.*
5. *Id.*
6. *Id.*
7. *Id.*
8. *Id.*
9. *Id.* at 436.
10. *Id.* at 432.

The Supreme Court did note that the United States, as amicus curiae, suggested a test for identifying the "article of manufacture."[11] This test included four factors: (1) the scope of design claimed in the plaintiff's patent, including the drawing and written description; (2) the relative prominence of the design within the product as a whole; (3) whether the design is conceptually distinct from the product as a whole; and (4) the physical relationship between the patented design and the rest of the product.[12]

District courts have adopted the preceding test to identify the relative "article of manufacture."[13]

---

11. *Id.* at 436.

12. Brief for the United States as Amicus Curiae Supporting Neither Party, *Samsung Electronics Co., Ltd. v. Apple, Inc.* (No. 15-777), at 27–29.

13. *See, e.g.*, MCP IP, LLC v. [PG].30-06 Outdoors, LLC & Daibow Inc., 643 F. Supp. 3d 800, 803 (2022).

Chapter 8
Apportionment

Regardless of the form, "a patentee must take care to seek only those damages attributable to the infringing feature" and "must in every case give evidence tending to separate or apportion the defendant's profits and the patentee's damages between the patented feature and unpatented features, and such evidence must be reliable and tangible, and not conjectural or speculative."[1]

The essential requirement of apportionment is that monetary relief, regardless of the form, "must reflect the value attributable to the infringing features of the product and no more."[2]

Chapters 5, 6, and 7 addressed the quantification of monetary relief by reference to lost profits, reasonable royalties, and the defendant's profits methodologies. This chapter addresses the apportionment of these monetary remedies and the Entire Market Value Rule, an exception to the apportionment requirement.

Apportionment Requirements

Lost Profits

Courts have accepted a "useful, but not exclusive" method of proving entitlement to lost profits, commonly called the Panduit Test.[3] The Panduit Test is a four-factor test. The first two Panduit Factors address apportionment in the context of a lost profits methodology.

1. Virtnetx, Inc. v. Cisco Sys., Inc., 767 F.3d 1308, 1326 (Fed. Cir. 2014) and Garretson v. Clark, 111 U.S. 120, 121 (Sup. Ct. 1884).

2. Ericsson, Inc. v. D-Link Sys., Inc., 773 F.3d 1201, 1226 (Fed. Cir. 2014).

3. Mentor Graphics Corp. v. EVE-USA, Inc., 851 F.3d 1275, 1284 (Fed Cir. 2017) (citing *Rite-Hite Corp.*, 56 F.3d at 1545) (citing Panduit Corp. v. Stahlin Bros. Fibre Works, Inc., 575 F.2d 1152 (6th Cir. 1978)).

Panduit Factor No. 1 requires the patentee to prove that demand existed for the patented product.[4] The key phrase is "patented product." Panduit Factor No. 1 considers the demand for the product as a whole.[5] Panduit Factor No. 2 requires the patentee to prove the absence of non-infringing substitutes.[6]

There is a relationship between Panduit Factor Nos. 1 and 2. While the first Panduit Factor considers "the demand for the patented product as a whole," the second considers the "demand for particular limitations or features of the claimed invention."[7] The satisfaction of Panduit Factor Nos. 1 and 2 "ties lost profit damages to specific claim limitations and ensures that damages are commensurate with the value of the patented features."[8] The Federal Circuit left for another day whether a different methodology incorporates the apportionment requirement.[9]

Reasonable Royalties

The essential requirement of apportionment is "that the ultimate reasonable royalty award must be based on the incremental value that the patented invention adds to the end product."[10] Additionally, "[W]hat is taken from the owner of a utility patent (for the purposes of assessing damages under § 284) is only the patented technology, and so the value to be measured is only the value of the infringing features of an accused product."[11] So, in a multi-component product, "the governing rule is that the ultimate combination of royalty base and royalty rate must reflect the value attributable to the infringing features of the product and no

4. Panduit Corp. v. Stahlin Bros. Fibre Works, Inc., 575 F.2d 1152, 1156 (6th Cir. 1978).

5. Mentor Graphics Corp. v. Eve-USA, Inc., 851 F.3d 1275, 1285 (Fed. Cir. 2017) (citing DePuy Spine, Inc. v. Medtronic Sofamor Danek, Inc., 567 F.3d 1314, 1330–31 (Fed. Cir. 2009).

6. *Panduit Corp.*, 575 F.2d at 1156.

7. *Mentor Graphics*, 851 F.3d at 1285.

8. *Id.*

9. *Id.* at 1288.

10. Ericsson, Inc. v. D-Link Sys., Inc., 773 F.3d 1201, 1226 (Fed. Cir. 2014).

11. *Id.*

more."[12] Otherwise, "the patentee will be improperly compensated for non-infringing components of that product."[13]

As a result, the court generally requires that "royalties be based not on the entire product, but instead on the 'smallest salable patent-practicing unit.'"[14] In other words, "the smallest salable patent-practicing unit principal states that a damages model cannot reliably apportion from a royalty base without that base being the smallest salable patent-practicing unit."[15]

However, "the requirement that a patentee identify damages associated with the smallest salable patent-practicing unit is simply a step toward meeting the requirement of apportionment."[16] When "the smallest salable infringing unit is, in fact, a multi-component product containing several non-infringing features with no relation to the patented feature, the patentee must do more to estimate what portion of the value of that product is attributable to the patented technology."[17]

Royalty Base or Royalty Rate?

Arithmetically, apportionment could occur by adjusting the royalty base or rate. As noted by the Federal Circuit:[18]

> Logically, an economist could do this in various ways—by careful selection of the royalty base to reflect the value added by the patented feature, where that differentiation is possible; by adjustment of the royalty rate so as to discount the value of a product's nonpatented features; or by a combination thereof. The essential requirement is that the ultimate reasonable royalty award must be based on the incremental value that the patented invention adds to the end product.

---

12. *Id.* at 1228.
13. LaserDynamics, Inc. v. Quanta Comput. USA, Inc., 694 F.3d 51, 67 (Fed. Cir. 2012).
14. *Id.*
15. Commonwealth Sci. & Indus. Rsch. Org. v. Cisco Sys., Inc., 809 F.3d 1295, 1302 (Fed. Cir. (2015).
16. Virnetx, Inc. v. Cisco Sys., Inc., 767 F.3d 1308, 1327 (Fed. Cir. 2014).
17. *Id.* at 1327–28.
18. Ericsson, Inc. v. D-Link Sys., Inc., 773 F.3d 1201, 1226 (Fed. Cir. 2014).

However, the Federal Circuit has warned against apportioning the royalty rate because of an "important evidentiary principle," the point of which:[19]

> is to help our jury system reliably implement the substantive statutory requirement of apportionment of royalty damages to the invention's value. The principle, applicable specifically to the choice of a royalty base, is that, where a multi-component product is at issue and the patented feature is not the item which imbues the combination of the other features with value, care must be taken to avoid misleading the jury by placing undue emphasis on the value of the entire product. It is not that an appropriately royalty award could never be fashioned by starting with the entire market value of a multi-component product-by, for instance, dramatically reducing the royalty rate to be applied in those cases—it is that reliance on the entire market value might mislead the jury, who may be less equipped to understand the extent to which the royalty rate would need to do the work in such instances.

While apportionment through the royalty base is more common, the Federal Circuit did approve a damages analysis apportioned through the royalty rate in *Exmark Manufacturing Co. Inc. v. Briggs & Stratton Power Products Group, LLC.*[20] The Federal Circuit noted that apportionment "can be done . . . through a thorough and reliable analysis to apportion the royalty rate."[21] They noted that a possible way to do this was through "a proper analysis of the *Georgia-Pacific* factors."[22]

Defendant's Profits

As addressed in Chapter 7, the quantification of the defendant's profits under 35 U.S.C. § 289 is a two-step process: (1) identification of the "article of manufacture" to which the infringed design was applied, and

19. *Id.* at 1226–27.

20. Exmark Mfg. Co. Inc. v. Briggs & Stratton Power Products Grp., LLC, 879 F.3d 1332 (Fed. Cir. 2018).

21. *Id.* at 1348–49.

22. *Id.* at 1349.

(2) calculating the "total profit" earned on that "article of manufacture."[23] As noted by the Supreme Court, the relevant "article of manufacture" was not the end product, but could be a component of the end product. Therefore, apportionment occurs with the identification of the "article of manufacture."

23. Samsung Elec. Co., Ltd. v. Apple Inc., 137 S. Ct. 429, 434 (2016).

Chapter 9
Income Statement

Regardless of the form, quantifying monetary relief arising from patent infringement requires an analysis of the revenue, expenses, and profit earned by the defendant's infringement, and the plaintiff's use of the patent in suit. Understanding the income statement is an essential component in quantifying the preceding.

An income statement includes revenues and expenses. Revenues are "sales of products, merchandise, and services, and earnings from interest, dividend[s], and rents."[1] An expense is "something spent on a specific item or for a particular purposes."[2] The purpose of an income statement is to summarize "the effect of revenues and expenses over time."[3]

A company may have numerous income statements, which serve different purposes. These income statements are layered and flow from a company's original book of entry, the general ledger. The general ledger is the "collection of all asset, liability owners equity, revenue and expense accounts."[4] The general ledger is like a checkbook and shows individual revenue and expense transactions.

1. New York State Society of CPAs Accounting Terminology Guide.
2. *Id.*
3. *Id.*
4. *Id.*

The following presents a company's general ledger for January 2025.

General Ledger: Jan. 2025					
Date	Description	Account	Account Type	Debit	Credit
1/2/2025	Receipt from Customer	Cash	Asset	10,000	
1/2/2025	Sale of Product	Revenue	Revenue		10,000
1/5/2025	Jan. Rent	Rent	Expense	2,500	
1/5/2025	Rent Payment	Cash	Asset		2,500
1/15/2025	Jan. Payroll	Payroll	Expense	5,500	
1/15/2025	Payment of Payroll	Cash	Asset		5,500
1/25/2025	Jan. Water Bill	Utilities	Expense	350	
1/25/2025	Payment of Water Bill	Cash	Asset		350

A trial balance summarizes the total debit and credit balances for each asset, liability, equity, revenue, and expense account on the general ledger. The trial balance ensures that the total debits equal the total credits.

Based on the general ledger from the preceding illustration, the following presents the company's trial balance for January 2025.

Trial Balance. Jan. 2025		
Account	Debit	Credit
Cash	1,650	
Revenue		10,000
Rent	2,500	
Payroll	5,500	
Utilities	350	
Total	10,000	10,000

The trial balance is often used as the starting point for preparing a financial statement. A company may prepare different income statements at various levels for specific decision-making purposes.

Levels of income statements may include (1) company, (2) division, and (3) product line.

The following sections address the income statement levels in greater detail and provide some guidance when quantifying patent damages.

Levels of Income Statements

Company Level

A company-level income statement presents the total effect of revenue and expenses over a period of time. It is the broadest level of a financial statement.

The following illustration presents a basic company-level income statement for Apex Corporation.

Income Statement: Company-Wide	
	2025
Revenue	$ 25,000,000
COGS	$ 12,500,000
Gross Profit	$ 12,500,000
Operating Expenses	
Selling, General, & Administrative	$ 5,000,000
Research & Development	$ 2,500,000
Other	$ 1,000,000
Total Operating Expenses	$ 8,500,000
Operating Profit	$ 4,000,000

Company-level financial statements can be prepared internally by management or externally by a Certified Public Accountant (CPA). A CPA can perform a Compilation, Review, or Audit of a company's financial statements. In a Compilation, a CPA is not required to verify the accuracy or completeness of the information in the financial statements and therefore offers no assurance.[5] In a Review, a CPA performs "analytical procedures, inquiries and other procedures to obtain 'limited assurance' on the financial statements and is intended to provide a user with a level of comfort on their accuracy."[6] An Audit provides the highest level of assurance.[7] In an Audit, a CPA "performs procedures in order to obtain 'reasonable assurance' (defined as a high but not absolute level of

5. AICPA Guide to Financial Statement Services: Compilation, Review, and Audit, at 4.
6. *Id.* at 6.
7. *Id.* at 7.

assurance) about whether the financial statements are free from material misstatement."[8]

Division Level

What if Apex Company had two divisions? In this case, management may want an income statement for each division. So, the company-level income statement is expanded to provide additional detail at the divisional level.

The following illustration presents a basic divisional-level income statement for Apex Company.

Income Statement: Divisional			
	2025		
	Division A	**Division B**	**Company Wide**
Revenue	$ 10,000,000	$ 15,000,000	$ 25,000,000
COGS	$ 5,000,000	$ 7,500,000	$ 12,500,000
Gross Profit	$ 5,000,000	$ 7,500,000	$ 12,500,000
Operating Expenses			
Selling, General, & Administrative	$ 1,500,000	$ 3,500,000	$ 5,000,000
Research & Development	$ 1,250,000	$ 1,250,000	$ 2,500,000
Other	$ 300,000	$ 700,000	$ 1,000,000
Total Operating Expenses	$ 3,050,000	$ 5,450,000	$ 8,500,000
Operating Profit	$ 1,950,000	$ 2,050,000	$ 4,000,000

Product Level

What if Division B of Apex Company had two products? Apex Company's division-level income statement could be further expanded at the product level.

The following illustration presents a basic product-level income statement for Division B of Apex Company.

8. *Id.*

Income Statement: Product Level			
	2025		
	Product 1	**Product 2**	**Division B**
Revenue	$ 10,000,000	$ 5,000,000	$ 15,000,000
COGS	$ 5,000,000	$ 2,500,000	$ 7,500,000
Gross Profit	$ 5,000,000	$ 2,500,000	$ 7,500,000
Operating Expenses			
Selling, General, & Administrative	$ 2,000,000	$ 1,500,000	$ 3,500,000
Research & Development	$ 1,000,000	$ 250,000	$ 1,250,000
Other	$ 600,000	$ 100,000	$ 700,000
Total Operating Expenses	$ 3,600,000	$ 1,850,000	$ 5,450,000
Operating Profit	$ 1,400,000	$ 650,000	$ 2,050,000

Patent Damages Guidance

The quantification of damages resulting from patent infringement often requires information and data from the income statements of the patentee and the infringer, including sales and profitability. As an example, let's consider what information would be required from the infringer to quantify reasonable royalty damages. This would include sales and profitability of the infringing product.[9]

When considering what documents to request, it is helpful to consider income statement levels. Progress from the broad to the specific. Does the company only sell one product? If so, then company-level financial statements may suffice to establish the sales of the infringing product. What if the company sells more than one product? Then, divisional or product-level income statements may be required. What if the company does not maintain product-level income statements? Then, the original books of entry or sales invoices for the infringing product may be required.

When considering profitability, some issues may arise. For example, a company may only track gross and not operating profits at the product

9. Georgia-Pacific Factor 8 addresses the established profitability of the product.

level. Gross profit is the difference between revenue and COGS (cost of goods sold). In this case, the other operating costs related to the infringing sales may need to be allocated from a broader income statement (i.e., division or company level). When a company allocates costs, it is important to discuss the cost allocation method and whether it makes sense in the context of a damages analysis.

The preceding are simplified examples. But understanding how a company's income statements are layered will help guide information requests to ensure the best available information is received.

Chapter 10
Patent Valuation

Three valuation approaches provide a general way to determine a value indication of a patent. Each valuation approach includes valuation methods, which provide specific ways to determine value.

Determining a reasonable royalty shares similarities with a fair market valuation of a patent. A general understanding of patent valuation theory provides a helpful framework for quantifying patent damages using a reasonable royalty methodology.

Cost Approach

Cost Approach and Methods

The Cost Approach is based on the premise that a prudent investor would pay no more for a patent than its replacement or reproduction cost. Two methods under the Cost Approach are the Reproduction Cost New Method and the Replacement Cost New Method. These methods are reduced for obsolescence to arrive at an indication of value.

Reproduction Cost New Method

The Reproduction Cost New Method determines an indication of value based on "the estimated cost to construct, at current prices, as of the date of analysis, an exact duplicate or replica of the subject intangible asset, using the same materials, production standards, design, layout, and quality of workmanship as the subject intangible asset."[1]

---

1. Robert F. Reilly & Robert P. Schweihs, Valuing Intangible Assets 122 (McGraw Hill, 1998).

Replacement Cost New Method

The Replacement Cost New Method determines an indication of value based on "estimated cost to construct, at current prices as of the date of the analysis, an intangible asset with equivalent utility to the subject intangible, using modern materials, production standards, design, layout, and quality of workmanship."[2]

Obsolescence

The Cost Approach Methods are reduced for obsolescence to arrive at an indication of value. Types of obsolescence considered for a patent are functional, technological, and economic.[3]

Functional obsolescence "is the reduction in the value of an intangible asset due to its inability to perform the function (or yield the economic utility) for which it was originally designed."[4] Functional obsolescence occurs when additional costs are incurred to use the intangible asset rather than current, superior alternatives.[5] Technical obsolescence "is a decrease in the value of an intangible asset due to improvements in technology."[6] Economic obsolescence occurs when the use of the subject intangible asset cannot provide an adequate return on investment.[7]

Applicability to Reasonable Royalty Methodology

The hypothetical negotiation approach incorporates concepts from the Cost Approach in Georgia-Pacific Factor 9, which addresses:[8]

> The utility and advantages of the patent property over the old modes or devices, if any, that had been used for working out similar results.

---

2. *Id.*
3. *Id.* at 127–28.
4. *Id.* at 127.
5. *Id.* at 127–28.
6. *Id.* at 128.
7. *Id.*
8. Georgia-Pacific Corp. v. U.S. Plywood Corp., 318 F. Supp. 1116, 1120 (1970).

Generally, the cost of switching to a non-infringing technology sets the ceiling of a licensing negotiation. All things equal, a licensee will not pay a royalty that exceeds the cost of (1) obtaining a non-infringing substitute or (2) designing around the patent in question.

Income Approach

Income Approach and Methods

The Income Approach establishes value based on a portion of the present value of the future economic benefits that accrue to the licensee. The Income Approach focuses on the patent's income-producing capability. The underlying premise of this approach is that the value of a patent can be measured by the present value of the net economic benefits it generates over its life.

Two methods under the Income Approach are the Discounted Cash Flow Method and the Capitalization of Earnings Method.

Discounted Cash Flow Method

The Discounted Cash Flow Method provides an indication of value by calculating the present value of a patent's expected future net cash flows using a discount rate. This method is used when future net cash flows are not expected to be constant over the patent's remaining life. At the most basic level, the Discounted Cash Flow Method requires three inputs: (1) the patent's expected future net cash flows, (2) the remaining life of the patent, and (3) a discount rate.

The following illustration provides a simplified example of the Discounted Cash Flow Method.

Discounted Cash Flow Method Example					
		Patent's Remaining Life			
		Year 1	**Year 2**	**Year 3**	**Year 4**
Revenue		$ 100,000	$ 150,000	$ 200,000	$ 250,000
COGS		$ 50,000	$ 75,000	$ 100,000	$ 125,000
Gross Profit		$ 50,000	$ 75,000	$ 100,000	$ 125,000
Operating Expenses		$ 20,000	$ 30,000	$ 40,000	$ 50,000

Discounted Cash Flow Method Example *(continued)*					
		Patent's Remaining Life			
		Year 1	**Year 2**	**Year 3**	**Year 4**
EBIT		$ 30,000	$ 45,000	$ 60,000	$ 75,000
Related to Patent		20.0%	20.0%	20.0%	20.0%
EBIT Related to Patent		$ 6,000	$ 9,000	$ 12,000	$ 15,000
Income Taxes	26.5%	$ 1,590	$ 2,385	$ 3,180	$ 3,975
Net Cash Flow Related to Patent		$ 4,410	$ 6,615	$ 8,820	$ 11,025
Discount Periods		0.50	1.50	2.50	3.50
Discount Rate	18.0%	0.9206	0.7801	0.6611	0.5603
Present Value		$ 4,060	$ 5,160	$ 5,831	$ 6,177
Indicated Value of Patent					$ 21,228

Capitalization of Earnings Method

The Capitalization of Earnings Method determines an indication of value by converting the economic benefits of an intangible asset for a single period using a capitalization rate. The capitalization rate represents the discount rate less the long-term sustainable growth rate. The Capitalization of Earnings Method is used when future net cash flows are expected to be constant over the remaining life of the patent.

The following illustration provides a simplified example of the Capitalization of Earnings Method.

Capitalization of Earnings Method		
		Amount
Revenue		$ 200,000
COGS		$ 100,000
Gross Profit		$ 100,000
Operating Expenses		$ 50,000
EBIT		$ 50,000
Related to Patent		20.0%
EBIT Related to Patent		$ 10,000
Income Taxes	26.5%	$ 2,650
Net Cash Flow Related to Patent		$ 7,350
Capitalization Factor		2.9220
Indicated Value of Patent		$ 21,477

The capitalization factor in the preceding example is based on (1) an 18 percent discount rate, (2) four years remaining life, and (3) midyear discounting convention. The Capitalization of Earnings Method is a mathematical shortcut when the net cash flows related to the patent are expected to be the same for every period. As shown in the following illustration, the Discounted Cash Flow Method with constant net cash flows yields the same value indication.

Discounted Cash Flow Method (Constant Net Cash Flows)					
		Patent's Remaining Life			
		Year 1	**Year 2**	**Year 3**	**Year 4**
Revenue		$ 200,000	$ 200,000	$ 200,000	$ 200,000
COGS		$ 100,000	$ 100,000	$ 100,000	$ 100,000
Gross Profit		$ 100,000	$ 100,000	$ 100,000	$ 100,000
Operating Expenses		$ 50,000	$ 50,000	$ 50,000	$ 50,000
EBIT		$ 50,000	$ 50,000	$ 50,000	$ 50,000
Related to Patent		20.0%	20.0%	20.0%	20.0%
EBIT Related to Patent		$ 10,000	$ 10,000	$ 10,000	$ 10,000
Income Taxes	26.5%	$ 2,650	$ 2,650	$ 2,650	$ 2,650
Net Cash Flow Related to Patent		$ 7,350	$ 7,350	$ 7,350	$ 7,350
Discount Periods (Midyear Convention)		0.50	1.50	2.50	3.50
Discount Rate	18.0%	0.9206	0.7801	0.6611	0.5603
Present Value		$ 6,766	$ 5,734	$ 4,859	$ 4,118
Indicated Value of Patent					$ 21,477

Applicability to Reasonable Royalty Methodology

The analytical method and hypothetical negotiation approach incorporate concepts from the Income Approach.

Analytical Method

The analytical method attempts to isolate the excess profit attributable to the patented invention and provide a portion of those excess profits to the patent owner in the form of a royalty. The analytical method requires (1) an analysis of the infringer's expected or projected profits at the time of infringement, and (2) a determination of the benchmark earnings retained by the infringer before the allocation of any excess profits to the patent owner (i.e., economic contribution of the patented technology).

Hypothetical Negotiation Approach

Under the hypothetical negotiation approach, Georgia-Pacific Factors 6, 8, 11, and 13 address the patent-in-suit's profitability and benefits. Georgia-Pacific Factor 6 addresses the economic effect of income generated from convoyed sales. Georgia-Pacific Factor 8 addresses the profitability and commercial success of the patented product. Georgia-Pacific Factor 11 addresses the value the infringer derives from the use of the patented technology. And Georgia-Pacific Factor 13 addresses the portion of the profit that should be credited to the invention.

Market Approach

Market Approach and Methods

The Market Approach establishes value through an analysis of comparable transactions.

The Market Approach measures value based on what other purchasers in the market have paid for a patent comparable to the subject patent. Two methods under the Market Approach are the Sales Transaction Method and the Relief from Royalty Method.[9]

Sales Transaction Method

The Sales Transaction Method determines an indication of value based on actual market transactions involving patents comparable to the subject patent. Adjustments may be made to the data to compensate for differences between the subject patent and reasonably similar patents.

Relief from Royalty Method

The Relief from Royalty Method accounts for the forgone expense of licensing an intangible asset in the absence of ownership. The application of the Relief from Royalty Method requires the identification of comparable royalty rates.

The following illustration provides a simplified example of the Relief from Royalty Method.

9. The Relief from Royalty Method is also referred to as a method under the Income Approach.

Relief from Royalty Method Example					
		Patent's Remaining Life			
		Year 1	**Year 2**	**Year 3**	**Year 4**
Revenue		$ 100,000	$ 150,000	$ 200,000	$ 250,000
Estimated Royalty Savings	5.0%	$ 5,000	$ 7,500	$ 10,000	$ 12,500
Income Taxes	26.5%	$ 1,325	$ 1,988	$ 2,650	$ 3,313
Net Royalty Savings		$ 3,675	$ 5,512	$ 7,350	$ 9,187
Discount Periods (Midyear Convention)		0.50	1.50	2.50	3.50
Discount Rate	18.0%	0.9206	0.7801	0.6611	0.5603
Present Value		$ 3,383	$ 4,300	$ 4,859	$ 5,147
Indicated Value of Patent					$ 17,689

Applicability to Reasonable Royalty Methodology

The established royalty and hypothetical negotiation approaches incorporate concepts from the Market Approach.

Established Royalty Approach

The established royalty approach bases a reasonable royalty on established royalties for the patent in suit. Like the Market Approach, it relies on comparable licensing transactions.

Hypothetical Negotiation Approach

Under the hypothetical negotiation approach, Georgia-Pacific Factors 1, 2, and 12 address market comparable royalties. Georgia-Pacific Factor 1 addresses royalty rates paid for the patent in suit. Georgia-Pacific Factor 2 addresses the royalty rates paid for patents comparable to the patent-in-suit. And Georgia-Pacific Factor 12 addresses the portion of the profit or of the selling price that may be customary in the particular business or in comparable businesses to allow for the use of the invention or analogous inventions.

Chapter 11
Discount Rates

A component of the Discounted Cash Flow Method under the Income Approach is the discount rate. A discount rate is a mechanism for assessing risk and determining its effect on the value of projected or future profits.

Understanding the discount rate for a patent begins with considering the company's overall discount rate. The weighted average cost of capital (WACC) is a method for developing a discount rate. The company's overall discount rate is comprised of all its tangible and intangible assets, which have different risk profiles. Therefore, the discount for a patent may differ from the company's overall discount rate.

WACC

The WACC is "the cost of capital (discount rate) determined by the weighted average, at market value, of the cost of all financing sources in the business enterprise's capital structure."[1] To calculate the WACC, you multiply the cost of equity for the subject company by the percentage or weight of equity in the capital structure, and then add the cost of debt for the subject company multiplied by the percentage or weight of debt in the capital structure.

1. International Glossary of Business Valuation Terms.

The following illustration sets out the WACC formula.

WACC Formula
WACC = (Ke * e%) + (Kd * d%)
Where:
Ke = Cost or Return on Equity
e% = Equity/Total Invested Capital
Kd = After-Tax Rate of Return on Debt
d% = Debt/Total Invested Capital

Cost of Equity

The build-up method can be used to calculate the cost of equity. The build-up method calculates the cost of equity by summing the systematic and unsystematic risks of a particular company. The components of the build-up method include (1) a risk-free rate (i.e., no risk of default), (2) an equity risk premium (i.e., premium investors must receive to invest in public equity instead of risk-free securities), (3) a size premium (i.e., risk of investing in a small versus large companies), and (4) a specific company risk factor (i.e., risks specific to the company).

The following illustration sets out an example calculation of the equity discount rate.

Development of Discount Rate (Cost of Equity Capital)	
Ke = Cost of equity capital (Rounded)	18.00%
Ke = Rf + RPm+ RPs + a	
Where:	
Rf = Risk-free rate	3.81%
RPm = Equity risk premium	7.17%
RPs = Size Premium	4.83%
a = Specific company risk	2.00%

Cost of Debt

The return on debt capital is the rate a prudent investor would require on interest-bearing debt. Since interest is tax deductible, the cost of debt should be net of taxes.

Company Versus Patent Discount Rates

The rates of return for individual assets differ. The required rates of return for an individual asset must be consistent with the relevant risk of investing in it. For example, cash is a low-risk asset, so the required rates of return will be lower than those for accounts receivable, which carry additional collection risk. Intangible assets, such as patents, are typically considered one of the riskier assets. On a weighted basis, the aggregate required rates of return on the individual assets should equal the WACC.

The following illustration is an example of the calculation of the weighted-average rates of return for a company's assets.

Asset	Market Value	Percent of Total	Rate of Return	Weighted Rate of Return
Working Capital	$ 30	7.3%	5.0%	0.4%
Accounts Receivable	$ 50	12.2%	8.0%	1.0%
Inventory	$ 200	48.8%	12.0%	5.9%
Fixed Assets	$ 50	12.2%	8.0%	1.0%
Patent	$ 80	19.5%	18.0%	3.5%
	$ 410	100.0%		11.7%

Chapter 12
Pre-Judgment Interest Concepts

Damages for patent infringement may include pre-judgment interest. Black's Law Dictionary defines pre-judgment interest as the "[S]tatutorily prescribed interest accrued either from the date of loss or from the date when the complaint was filed up to the date the final judgment is entered." The court has discretion over the interest rate and compounding periods used to quantify pre-judgment interest. These factors may have a sizable impact on the amount of a pre-judgment interest award.

Simple Versus Compounded Interest

To understand the difference between simple and compounded interest, consider the following example. Let's assume that the plaintiff prevailed against the defendant for patent infringement, and the court awarded damages totaling $10,000,000. The following illustration sets out the preceding damages by year.

Damage Award	
Damage Period	**Damages**
1	500,000
2	750,000
3	1,000,000
4	2,000,000
5	2,500,000
6	3,250,000
Total	10,000,000

The court also awarded pre-judgment interest at 5 percent from the beginning of the damage period to the date of the judgment at the end of year seven.

Simple Interest

Let's assume that the court mandated that pre-judgment interest be calculated using simple interest. Simple interest is only calculated on the initial damages.

The following illustration sets out the simple interest formula.

Simple Interest Formula
SI = P × i × n
Where:
SI = Simple Interest
P = Principal
i = Interest Rate
n = Periods

The following illustration calculates the simple interest on the $10,000,000 damage award using a 5 percent interest rate.

Pre-Judgment Interest (Simple Interest Calculation)					
Damage Period	**Damages**	**Interest Rate**	**Interest per Year**	**Years to Judgment**	**Pre-Judgment Interest**
1	$ 500,000	5.0%	$ 25,000	6.0	$ 150,000
2	$ 750,000	5.0%	$ 37,500	5.0	$ 187,500
3	$ 1,000,000	5.0%	$ 50,000	4.0	$ 200,000
4	$ 2,000,000	5.0%	$ 100,000	3.0	$ 300,000
5	$ 2,500,000	5.0%	$ 125,000	2.0	$ 250,000
6	$ 3,250,000	5.0%	$ 162,500	1.0	$ 162,500
Total	$ 10,000,000				$ 1,250,000

As noted earlier, pre-judgment interest was $1.25 million using a simple interest calculation.

Compounded Interest

Now, let's assume that the court mandated that pre-judgment interest be calculated using compounded interest. Compounded interest is calculated on the initial damages and interest.

The following illustration sets out the compound interest formula.

Compound Interest Formula
CI = (P(1+i)^n)-P
Where:
CI = Compound Interest
P = Principal
i = Interest Rate
n = Periods

The following illustration calculates the compound interest on the $10,000,000 damage award using a 5 percent interest rate.

Pre-Judgment Interest (Compound Interest Calculation)						
Damage Period	**Initial Damages**	**Interest Rate (Annual)**	**Periods (Years)**	**Future Value Interest Factor**	**Future Value**	**Pre-Judgment Interest**
[1]	[2]	[3]	[4]	[5]=(1+[3])^[4]	[6]=[2]×[5]	[7] = [6]–[2]
1	$ 500,000	5.0%	6.0	1.3401	$ 670,048	$ 170,048
2	$ 750,000	5.0%	5.0	1.2763	$ 957,211	$ 207,211
3	$ 1,000,000	5.0%	4.0	1.2155	$ 1,215,506	$ 215,506
4	$ 2,000,000	5.0%	3.0	1.1576	$ 2,315,250	$ 315,250
5	$ 2,500,000	5.0%	2.0	1.1025	$ 2,756,250	$ 256,250
6	$ 3,250,000	5.0%	1.0	1.0500	$ 3,412,500	$ 162,500
Total	$ 10,000,000					$ 1,326,765

As noted earlier, pre-judgment interest was $1.33 million using a compounded interest calculation, which is over 6.4 percent higher than the simple interest calculation.

Impact of Compounding

The number of compounding periods may also significantly affect the size of a pre-judgment interest award. Following the same example, the following illustration demonstrates the impact of compounding periods on a pre-judgment interest calculation.

Impact of Compounding Periods						
		Pre-Judgment Interest				
Damage Period	**Initial Damages**	**Yearly Compounding**	**Quarterly Compounding**	**Monthly Compounding**	**Daily Compounding**
1	$ 500,000	$ 170,048	$ 173,676	$ 174,509	$ 174,916
2	$ 750,000	$ 207,211	$ 211,528	$ 212,519	$ 213,003
3	$ 1,000,000	$ 215,506	$ 219,890	$ 220,895	$ 221,386
4	$ 2,000,000	$ 315,250	$ 321,509	$ 322,944	$ 323,645
5	$ 2,500,000	$ 256,250	$ 261,215	$ 262,353	$ 262,908
6	$ 3,250,000	$ 162,500	$ 165,572	$ 166,276	$ 166,619
Total	$ 10,000,000	$ 1,326,765	$ 1,353,390	$ 1,359,496	$ 1,362,477

As noted earlier, all else equal, the greater the number of compounding periods, the greater the pre-judgment interest.

Chapter 13
Purchase Price Allocations

Financial reporting rules related to "purchase price allocations" may provide helpful information related to the quantification of damages using a reasonable royalty methodology. Purchase price allocations may contain information on comparable royalty rates and potentially assist with apportionment.

What Are Purchase Price Allocations?

FASB Accounting Standards Codification (ASC) 805, entitled Business Combinations, "provides guidance on the accounting and reporting for business combinations to be accounted for under the acquisition method."[1]

Per ASC 805, the acquisition method:[2]

> reflects the overall principle that when an entity (the acquirer) obtains control of a business (the acquiree), the acquirer generally recognizes and measures the assets acquired and liabilities assumed at their fair values as of the date that control is obtained, thereby establishing a new accounting basis for the acquiree.

On the acquisition date, the acquirer recognizes (on the balance sheet) separately from goodwill the identifiable assets acquired, the liabilities assumed, and any non-controlling interest in the acquiree at fair value.[3] This is referred to as a purchase price allocation.

---

1. AICPA Accounting and Valuation Guide: Business Combinations, at 11 (2024).
2. *Id.*
3. *Id.* at 13.

Identifiable assets include intangible assets.[4] The FASB ASC Master Glossary defines intangible assets as "assets (not including financial assets) that lack physical substance (the term intangible assets is used to refer to intangible assets other than goodwill)."[5]

A purchase price allocation only includes intangible assets that are "identifiable."[6] An "identifiable" intangible asset must be (1) separable or (2) arise from contractual or other legal rights.[7] Categories of identifiable intangible assets include (1) marketing-related intangibles, (2) customer-related intangibles, (3) artistic-related intangibles, (4) contract-based intangible assets, and (5) technology-based intangibles.[8] Technology-based intangibles include patents.[9]

A purchase price allocation requires that identifiable assets be measured at fair value, which in turn requires a valuation.

Purchase Price Allocations and Reasonable Royalty Damages

What do purchase price allocations have to do with reasonable royalty damages? Let's consider the following example, which is loosely based on an actual transaction.[10]

On May 22, 2022, Google completed the acquisition of Motorola. Google expected that the acquisition would protect and advance its Android ecosystem and enhance its mobile computing capabilities. The purchase price was $12.5 billion. Google retained an independent valuation firm to perform the purchase price allocation summarized in the following illustration.

4. *Id.* at 77.
5. *Id.*
6. *Id.*
7. *Id.* at 78.
8. *Id.* at 82–83.
9. *Id.* at 92.
10. I based the example on an actual transaction. However, I used fictional amounts and other information for illustrative purposes.

Purchase Price Allocation: Motorola Acquisition		
(billions)	**Fair Value**	
Cash	$ 2.9	23.4%
Patent	$ 5.5	44.4%
Customer Relationships	$ 0.7	5.6%
Goodwill	$ 2.5	20.2%
Other Net Assets	$ 0.8	6.5%
Purchase Price	$ 12.4	100.0%

The independent valuation firm valued the patent acquired by Google at $5.5 billion using the Relief-from-Royalty Method under the Market Approach.

The following illustration sets out the valuation of the patent.

Relief from Royalty Method Example								
		Patent's Remaining Life						
(billions)		**Year 1**	**Year 2**	**Year 3**	**Year 4**	**Year 5**	**Year 6**	**Year 7**
Revenue		$ 20.00	$ 22.00	$ 24.00	$ 26.00	$ 28.00	$ 29.00	$ 30.00
Estimated Royalty Savings	7.4%	$ 1.48	$ 1.63	$ 1.77	$ 1.92	$ 2.07	$ 2.14	$ 2.22
Income Taxes	26.5%	0.39	0.43	0.47	0.51	0.55	0.57	0.59
Net Royalty Savings		$ 1.09	$ 1.20	$ 1.30	$ 1.41	$ 1.52	$ 1.57	$ 1.63
Discount Periods		0.50	1.50	2.50	3.50	4.50	5.50	6.50
Discount Rate	18.0%	0.9206	0.7801	0.6611	0.5603	0.4748	0.4024	0.3410
Present Value		$ 1.00	$ 0.94	$ 0.86	$ 0.79	$ 0.72	$ 0.63	$ 0.56
Indicated Value of Patent								**$ 5.50**

Two years after the acquisition, Google filed suit alleging that Samsung infringed the patent it acquired from Motorola (Samsung Litigation).[11]

11. Hypothetical litigation for illustrative purposes only.

Purchase price allocations provide evidence related to royalty rates. In this example, an independent third-party valuation firm, outside of litigation, valued the subject patent using a concluded royalty rate of 7.4 percent. The financial statements, which included the purchase price allocation, were audited by an independent certified public accountant and submitted to the Securities and Exchange Commission. In this simplified example, the purchase price allocation provides third-party evidence, outside the context of litigation, of a reasonable royalty rate.

Purchase price allocations also apportion value. The purchase price allocation indicates that the subject patent accounted for 44.4 percent of the fair value purchase price. The preceding suggests that the patent's value represented over 44.0 percent of the company's total fair value. From an economic perspective, this is consistent with the concept of apportionment, that is, "that the ultimate reasonable royalty award must be based on the incremental value that the patented invention adds to the end product."[12] Accordingly, the 44.0 percent from the purchase price allocation may provide evidence related to apportionment in the context of reasonable royalty damages.

---

12. Ericsson, Inc. v. D-Link Sys., Inc., 773 F.3d 1201, 1226 (Fed. Cir. 2014).

Appendix 1
U.S.C Patent Remedy Sections

35 U.S.C. § 281—Remedy for Infringement

A patentee shall have remedy by civil action for infringement of his patent.

35 U.S.C. § 283—Injunction

The several courts having jurisdiction of cases under this title may grant injunctions in accordance with the principles of equity to prevent the violation of any right secured by patent, on such terms as the court deems reasonable.

35 U.S.C. § 284—Damages

Upon finding for the claimant the court shall award the claimant damages adequate to compensate for the infringement, but in no event less than a reasonable royalty for the use made of the invention by the infringer, together with interest and costs as fixed by the court.

When the damages are not found by a jury, the court shall assess them. In either event the court may increase the damages up to three times the amount found or assessed. Increased damages under this paragraph shall not apply to provisional rights under section 154(d).

The court may receive expert testimony as an aid to the determination of damages or of what royalty would be reasonable under the circumstances.

35 U.S.C. § 285—Attorney Fees

The court in exceptional cases may award reasonable attorney fees to the prevailing party.

35 U.S.C. § 286—Time Limitation on Damages

Except as otherwise provided by law, no recovery shall be had for any infringement committed more than six years prior to the filing of the complaint or counterclaim for infringement in the action.

In the case of claims against the United States Government for use of a patented invention, the period before bringing suit, up to six years, between the date of receipt of a written claim for compensation by the department or agency of the Government having authority to settle such claim, and the date of mailing by the Government of a notice to the claimant that his claim has been denied shall not be counted as part of the period referred to in the preceding paragraph.

35 U.S.C. § 287—Limitation on Damages and Other Remedies; Marking and Notice

(a) Patentees, and persons making, offering for sale, or selling within the United States any patented article for or under them, or importing any patented article into the United States, may give notice to the public that the same is patented, either by fixing thereon the word "patent" or the abbreviation "pat." together with the number of the patent, or by fixing thereon the word "patent" or the abbreviation "pat." together with an address of a posting on the Internet, accessible to the public without charge for accessing the address, that associates the patented article with the number of the patent, or when, from the character of the article, this can not be done, by fixing to it, or to the package wherein one or more of them is contained, a label containing a like notice. In the event of failure so to mark, no damages shall be recovered by the patentee in any action for infringement, except on proof that the infringer was notified of the infringement and continued to infringe thereafter, in which event damages may be recovered only for infringement occurring after such notice. Filing of an action for infringement shall constitute such notice.

(b)

(1) An infringer under section 271(g) shall be subject to all the provisions of this title relating to damages and injunctions except to the extent those remedies are modified by this subsection or section 9006 of the Process Patent Amendments Act of 1988. The modifications of remedies provided in this subsection shall not be available to any person who—

(A) practiced the patented process;

(B) owns or controls, or is owned or controlled by, the person who practiced the patented process; or

(C) had knowledge before the infringement that a patented process was used to make the product the importation, use, offer for sale, or sale of which constitutes the infringement.

(2) No remedies for infringement under section 271(g) shall be available with respect to any product in the possession of, or in transit to, the person subject to liability under such section before that person had notice of infringement with respect to that product. The person subject to liability shall bear the burden of proving any such possession or transit.

(3)

(A) In making a determination with respect to the remedy in an action brought for infringement under section 271(g), the court shall consider—

(i) the good faith demonstrated by the defendant with respect to a request for disclosure,

(ii) the good faith demonstrated by the plaintiff with respect to a request for disclosure, and

(iii) the need to restore the exclusive rights secured by the patent.

(B) For purposes of subparagraph (A), the following are evidence of good faith:

(i) a request for disclosure made by the defendant;

(ii) a response within a reasonable time by the person receiving the request for disclosure; and

(iii) the submission of the response by the defendant to the manufacturer, or if the manufacturer is not known, to the supplier, of the product to be purchased by the defendant, together with a request for a written statement that the process claimed in any patent disclosed in the response is not used to produce such product.

The failure to perform any acts described in the preceding sentence is evidence of absence of good faith unless there are mitigating circumstances. Mitigating circumstances include the case in which, due to the nature of the product, the number of sources for the product, or like commercial circumstances, a request for disclosure is not necessary or practicable to avoid infringement.

(4)

(A) For purposes of this subsection, a "request for disclosure" means a written request made to a person then engaged in the manufacture of a product to identify all process patents owned by or licensed to that person, as of the time of the request, that the person then reasonably believes could be asserted to be infringed under section 271(g) if that product were imported into, or sold, offered for sale, or used in, the United States by an unauthorized person. A request for disclosure is further limited to a request—

(i) which is made by a person regularly engaged in the United States in the sale of the same type of products as those manufactured by the person to whom the request is directed, or which includes facts showing that the person making the request plans to engage in the sale of such products in the United States;

(ii) which is made by such person before the person's first importation, use, offer for sale, or sale of units of the product produced by an infringing process and before the person had notice of infringement with respect to the product; and

(iii) which includes a representation by the person making the request that such person will promptly submit the patents identified pursuant to the request to the manufacturer, or if the manufacturer is not known, to the supplier, of the product to be purchased by the person making the request, and will request from that manufacturer or supplier a written statement that none of the processes claimed in those patents is used in the manufacture of the product.

(B) In the case of a request for disclosure received by a person to whom a patent is licensed, that person shall either identify the patent or promptly notify the licensor of the request for disclosure.

(C) A person who has marked, in the manner prescribed by subsection (a), the number of the process patent on all products made by the patented process which have been offered for sale or sold by that person in the United States, or imported by the person into the United States, before a request for disclosure is received is not required to respond to the request for disclosure. For purposes of the preceding sentence, the term "all products" does not include products made before the effective date of the Process Patent Amendments Act of 1988.

(5)

(A) For purposes of this subsection, notice of infringement means actual knowledge, or receipt by a person of a written notification, or a combination thereof, of information sufficient to persuade a reasonable person that it is likely that a product was made by a process patented in the United States.

(B) A written notification from the patent holder charging a person with infringement shall specify the patented process alleged to have been used and the reasons for a good faith belief that such process was used. The patent holder shall include in the notification such information as is reasonably necessary to explain fairly the patent holder's belief, except that the patent holder is not required to disclose any trade secret information.

(C) A person who receives a written notification described in subparagraph (B) or a written response to a request for disclosure described in paragraph (4) shall be deemed to have notice of infringement with respect to any patent referred to in such written notification or response unless that person, absent mitigating circumstances—

(i) promptly transmits the written notification or response to the manufacturer or, if the manufacturer is not known, to the supplier, of the product purchased or to be purchased by that person; and

(ii) receives a written statement from the manufacturer or supplier which on its face sets forth a well grounded factual basis for a belief that the identified patents are not infringed.

(D) For purposes of this subsection, a person who obtains a product made by a process patented in the United States in a quantity which is abnormally large in relation to the volume of business of such person or an efficient inventory level shall be rebuttably presumed to have actual knowledge that the product was made by such patented process.

(6) A person who receives a response to a request for disclosure under this subsection shall pay to the person to whom the request was made a reasonable fee to cover actual costs incurred in complying with the request, which may not exceed the cost of a commercially available automated patent search of the matter involved, but in no case more than $500.

(c)

(1) With respect to a medical practitioner's performance of a medical activity that constitutes an infringement under section 271(a) or (b), the provisions of sections 281, 283, 284, and 285 shall not

apply against the medical practitioner or against a related health care entity with respect to such medical activity.

(2) For the purposes of this subsection:

(A) the term "medical activity" means the performance of a medical or surgical procedure on a body, but shall not include (i) the use of a patented machine, manufacture, or composition of matter in violation of such patent, (ii) the practice of a patented use of a composition of matter in violation of such patent, or (iii) the practice of a process in violation of a biotechnology patent.

(B) the term "medical practitioner" means any natural person who is licensed by a State to provide the medical activity described in subsection (c)(1) or who is acting under the direction of such person in the performance of the medical activity.

(C) the term "related health care entity" shall mean an entity with which a medical practitioner has a professional affiliation under which the medical practitioner performs the medical activity, including but not limited to a nursing home, hospital, university, medical school, health maintenance organization, group medical practice, or a medical clinic.

(D) the term "professional affiliation" shall mean staff privileges, medical staff membership, employment or contractual relationship, partnership or ownership interest, academic appointment, or other affiliation under which a medical practitioner provides the medical activity on behalf of, or in association with, the health care entity.

(E) the term "body" shall mean a human body, organ or cadaver, or a nonhuman animal used in medical research or instruction directly relating to the treatment of humans.

(F) the term "patented use of a composition of matter" does not include a claim for a method of performing a medical or surgical procedure on a body that recites the use of a composition of matter where the use of that composition of matter does not directly contribute to achievement of the objective of the claimed method.

(G) the term "State" shall mean any State or territory of the United States, the District of Columbia, and the Commonwealth of Puerto Rico.

(3) This subsection does not apply to the activities of any person, or employee or agent of such person (regardless of whether such person is a tax exempt organization under section 501(c) of the Internal Revenue Code), who is engaged in the commercial development, manufacture, sale, importation, or distribution of a machine, manufacture, or composition of matter or the provision of pharmacy or clinical laboratory services (other than clinical laboratory services provided in a physician's office), where such activities are:

(A) directly related to the commercial development, manufacture, sale, importation, or distribution of a machine, manufacture, or composition of matter or the provision of pharmacy or clinical laboratory services (other than clinical laboratory services provided in a physician's office), and

(B) regulated under the Federal Food, Drug, and Cosmetic Act, the Public Health Service Act, or the Clinical Laboratories Improvement Act.

(4) This subsection shall not apply to any patent issued based on an application which has an effective filing date before September 30, 1996.

35 U.S.C. § 288—Action for Infringement of a Patent Containing an Invalid Claim

Whenever a claim of a patent is invalid, an action may be maintained for the infringement of a claim of the patent which may be valid. The patentee shall recover no costs unless a disclaimer of the invalid claim has been entered at the Patent and Trademark Office before the commencement of the suit.

35 U.S.C. § 289—Additional Remedy for Infringement of Design Patent

Whoever during the term of a patent for a design, without license of the owner, (1) applies the patented design, or any colorable imitation thereof, to any article of manufacture for the purpose of sale, or (2) sells or exposes for sale any article of manufacture to which such design or colorable imitation has been applied shall be liable to the owner to the extent of his total profit, but not less than $250, recoverable in any United States district court having jurisdiction of the parties.

Nothing in this section shall prevent, lessen, or impeach any other remedy which an owner of an infringed patent has under the provisions of this title, but he shall not twice recover the profit made from the infringement.

35 U.S.C. § 292—False Marking

(a) Whoever, without the consent of the patentee, marks upon, or affixes to, or uses in advertising in connection with anything made, used, offered for sale, or sold by such person within the United States, or imported by the person into the United States, the name or any imitation of the name of the patentee, the patent number, or the words "patent," "patentee," or the like, with the intent of counterfeiting or imitating the mark of the patentee, or of deceiving the public and inducing them to believe that the thing was made, offered for sale, sold, or imported into the United States by or with the consent of the patentee; or

Whoever marks upon, or affixes to, or uses in advertising in connection with any unpatented article, the word "patent" or any word or number importing that the same is patented, for the purpose of deceiving the public; or

Whoever marks upon, or affixes to, or uses in advertising in connection with any article, the words "patent applied for," "patent pending," or any word importing that an application for patent has been made, when no application for patent has been made, or if made, is not pending, for the purpose of deceiving the public—

Shall be fined not more than $500 for every such offense. Only the United States may sue for the penalty authorized by this subsection.
(b) A person who has suffered a competitive injury as a result of a violation of this section may file a civil action in a district court of the United States for recovery of damages adequate to compensate for the injury.
(c) The marking of a product, in a manner described in subsection (a), with matter relating to a patent that covered that product but has expired is not a violation of this section.

Appendix 2
Georgia-Pacific Factors

1. The royalties received by the patentee for the licensing of the patent in suit, proving or tending to prove an established royalty.
2. The rates paid by the licensee for the use of other patents comparable to the patent in suit.
3. The nature and scope of the license, as exclusive or non-exclusive; or as restricted or non-restricted in terms of territory or with respect to whom the manufactured product may be sold.
4. The licensor's established policy and marketing program to maintain his patent monopoly by not licensing others to use the invention or by granting licenses under special conditions designed to preserve that monopoly.
5. The commercial relationship between the licensor and licensee, such as, whether they are competitors in the same territory in the same line of business or whether they are inventor and promotor.
6. The effect of selling the patented specialty in promoting sales of other products of the licensee, the existing value of the invention to the licensor as a generator of sales of his non-patented items, and the extent of such derivative or convoyed sales.
7. The duration of the patent and the term of the license.
8. The established profitability of the product made under the patent, its commercial success, and its current popularity.
9. The utility and advantages of the patent property over the old modes or devices, if any, that had been used for working out similar results.
10. The nature of the patented invention, the character of the commercial embodiment of it as owned and produced by the licensor, and the benefits to those who have used the invention.

11. The extent to which the infringer has made use of the invention, and any evidence probative of the value of that use.
12. The portion of the profit or of the selling price that may be customary in the particular business or in comparable businesses to allow for the use of the invention or analogous inventions.
13. The portion of the realizable profit that should be credited to the invention as distinguished from non-patented elements, the manufacturing process, business risks, or significant features or improvements added by the infringer.
14. The opinion testimony of qualified experts.
15. The amount that a licensor (such as the patentee) and a licensee (such as the infringer) would have agreed upon (at the time the infringement began) if both had been reasonably and voluntarily trying to reach an agreement; that is, the amount that a prudent licensee—who desired, as a business proposition, to obtain a license to manufacture and sell a particular article embodying the patented invention—would have been willing to pay as a royalty and yet be able to make a reasonable profit and which amount would have been acceptable by a prudent patentee who was willing to grant a license.

Index

About the ABA Section of Intellectual Property Law

From its strength within the American Bar Association, the ABA Section of Intellectual Property Law (ABA-IPL) advances the development and improvement of intellectual property laws and their fair and just administration. The Section furthers the goals of its members by sharing knowledge and balanced insight on the full spectrum of intellectual property law and practice, including patents, trademarks, copyright, design, and trade secrets. Providing a forum for rich perspectives and reasoned commentary, ABA-IPL serves as the ABA voice of intellectual property law within the profession, before policy makers, and with the public.

Books from the ABA Section of Intellectual Property Law (ABA-IPL)

ABA AMERICAN BAR ASSOCIATION
Intellectual Property Law Section

Title	Regular Price	ABA-IPL Member Price
ADR Advocacy, Strategies, and Practices for Intellectual Property and Technology Cases, 3rd Ed. (5370273)	$179.95	**$144.95**
ANDA Litigation, 4th Ed. (5370274)	$395.00	**$355.00**
Antitrust Issues in Intellectual Property Law, 2nd Ed. (5370263)	$149.95	**$119.95**
Arbitrating Patent Disputes (5370229)	$89.95	**$74.95**
Biosimilars Litigation and Client Counseling (5370267)	$169.95	**$139.95**
Careers in IP Law (5370204) (The ebook is complimentary with ABA-IPL Section membership)	$24.95	**$16.95**
Commercialization of IP Rights in China (5370241)	$119.95	**$95.95**
A Comprehensive Patent Practice Form Book (5370260)	$139.95	**$109.95**
Computer Games and Immersive Entertainment, 2nd Ed. (5370239)	$89.95	**$69.95**
Copyright Litigation Strategies (5370228)	$369.00	**$285.00**
Copyright Remedies (5370208)	$89.95	**$74.95**
Crash Course on U.S. Patent Law (5370221)	$39.95	**$34.95**
The DMCA Handbook, 2nd Ed. (5370234)	$79.95	**$64.95**
The Essential Case Law Guide to PTAB Trials (5370233)	$249.95	**$199.95**
The Essentials of Japanese Patent Prosecution (5370245)	$149.95	**$119.95**
Intellectual Property and Technology Due Diligence (5370236)	$219.95	**$179.95**
The Intellectual Property Law Handbook, 2nd Ed. (5620154)	$139.95	**$109.95**
Introduction to Patent Litigation (5370277)	$99.95	**$79.95**
IP Protection in China, 2nd Ed. (5370270)	$149.95	**$119.95**
IP Strategies for Medical Device Technologies (5370238)	$149.95	**$119.95**
IP Valuation for the Future (5370237)	$89.95	**$59.95**
The Law of Trade Secret Litigation Under the Uniform Trade Secrets Act, 2nd Ed. (5370242)	$369.95	**$295.95**
A Lawyer's Guide to Section 337 Investigations before the U.S. International Trade Commission, 5th Ed. (5370266)	$139.95	**$109.95**
Legal Guide to Video Game Development, 2nd Ed. (5370227)	$74.95	**$59.95**
A Legal Strategist's Guide to Trademark Trial and Appeal Board Practice, 5th Ed. (5370275)	$179.95	**$144.95**
Marketing Your Invention, Product, or Journey, 4th Ed. (5370271)	$59.95	**$47.95**
New Practitioner's Guide to Intellectual Property (5370198)	$89.95	**$69.95**
Patent Claim Drafting Practice (5370259)	$179.95	**$144.95**
Patent Damages (5370276)	$79.95	**$64.95**

Title	Regular Price	ABA-IPL Member Price
Patent Freedom to Operate Searches, Opinions, Techniques, and Studies (5370230)	$139.95	**$109.95**
Patent Litigation Strategies Handbook, 5th Ed. (5370269)	$395.00	**$355.00**
Patent Trial Advocacy Casebook, 3rd Ed. (5370124)	$149.95	**$119.95**
Patently Persuasive, 2nd Ed. (5370272)	$139.95	**$119.95**
The Practitioner's Guide to the PCT, 2nd Ed. (5370261)	$139.95	**$109.95**
The Practitioner's Guide to Trials Before the Patent Trial and Appeal Board, 3rd Ed. (5370258)	$169.95	**$139.95**
Pre-ANDA Litigation, 3rd Ed. (5370256)	$349.00	**$259.00**
Preliminary Relief in Patent Infringement Disputes (5370194)	$119.95	**$94.95**
Principles of Patent Claim Drafting and Patent Claim Analysis (5370268)	$159.95	**$127.95**
Right of Publicity (5370215)	$89.95	**$74.95**
Settlement of Patent Litigation and Disputes (5370192)	$179.95	**$144.95**
Starting an IP Law Practice (5370202)	$54.95	**$34.95**
Summary of Covenants Not to Compete (5370244)	$179.95	**$144.95**
The Tech Contracts Handbook, 3rd Ed. (5370248)	$42.95	**$33.95**
Trademark and Deceptive Advertising Surveys, 2nd Ed. (5370255)	$189.95	**$151.95**
What Is a Copyright, 4th Ed. (5370257)	$19.95	**$16.95**
What Is a Patent, 4th Ed. (5370262)	$19.95	**$16.95**
What Is a Trademark, 5th Ed. (5370254)	$19.95	**$16.95**
What Is a Trade Secret (5370265)	$19.95	**$16.95**

Find these and other ABA-IPL books at ShopABA.com

Thank you for your order!

Jeff Salyards
Executive Editor, ABA Publishing
jeff.salyards@americanbar.org

Tax, shipping and handling charges may apply.
See web store for complete details and current shipping and handling rates and information.

2 EASY WAYS TO ORDER **ShopABA.org** OR **(800) 285-2221**

ABA-IPL Books Editorial Board
2025–26

Jeff Salyards
Executive Editor
ABA Publishing
jeff.salyards@americanbar.org